AMERICA, WORKING.

Book and Photographs by Linda Sullivan Schulte

NISH • VIENNA, VIRGINIA • 1998

Library of Congress Card Catalog
Number: 98-91280

ISBN No. 0-9663049-0-X

Dedication

To E. Richard Alley, Jr.

who brought courage,

honesty and strength to the

JWOD Program for 25 years

and

for those people with

disabilities everywhere who

are determined to find

success in the workplace

Contents

Foreword

There is a profound gulf in American society between "us" and "them," those who "have" and those who carry with them the enormous burdens of profound disabilities. "We" tend not to see or interact with "them" as America's urban neighborhoods and small town life have given way to suburbs, transience and the insularity of modern life.

The enormous value of the Javits-Wagner-O'Day Act—the federal law passed 60 years ago which directs federal procurement dollars towards those who are blind or severely disabled—is that it breaches this gap in our social fabric. It does so by recognizing that each of us can and must contribute his or her unique skills and energy toward the creation of a better society. All of us need a sense of purpose, that we are contributing to society. The JWOD Act provides opportunity for those who are most socially isolated and enables them to connect and contribute to us all. In addition, including "them" in the process of production "we" ourselves are provided a sense of purpose—the facilitation of full participation in our society by those who could otherwise remain shunned and excluded. The good that comes from the real productivity of those engaged under the Act itself pales in comparison with the social good.

My father, Senator Jacob K. Javits, authored the Amendment to the JWOD Act which added those with other severe disabilities to people who were blind who were the original beneficiaries of the program. In so doing, he reinvigorated the original purpose of the law—to help the most vulnerable members of society by including them as productive citizens through modest governmental efforts. He believed with Lincoln that: "The legitimate object of government is to do for a community of people whatever they need to have done, but cannot do at all, or cannot do so well in their separate and individual capacities. In all that people can do for themselves, the government ought not to interfere."

The JWOD Act is a great expression of what makes this nation unique in the world—the degree to which it cares about opening to each individual the opportunity to contribute to the extent of their capabilities. In this way, the individual good and the social good coincide. We are all the true beneficiaries of this law.

Joshua M. Javits
May 1998

Preface

There are no limits on human potential. That was the belief of Caroline O'Day, Robert Wagner and Jacob Javits when they lashed their names forever to the mast of federal procurement law in the singular hope of steering jobs in the direction of people who needed them most; people who are blind and who have other severe disabilities. It might also be said that these three legislators from New York believed something else too; that there are no limits on the ability of the federal government to serve people effectively if driven by discipline, reason and heart.

As a result of the passage of legislation sixty years ago, a little-known government program has created jobs for thousands of Americans nationwide. In 1997 alone, over thirty thousand people with severe disabilities were working on JWOD projects.

While the story of the Javits-Wagner-O'Day Program cannot be told in one tale—perhaps not even in sixty—this book hopefully offers a glimpse into the power of this program through the impact it has had on the lives of Americans with disabilities.

Along with that message, comes another. It is this: If given an opportunity, people with even the most severe disabilities imaginable can achieve independence and economic security through excellence in the workplace.

One of the stories in the pages that follow is about Clinton Montgomery in Kentucky. Clinton, who has mental retardation, loved his job making tool boxes for the General Services Administration so much that he tried never to miss a day. Clinton, with no driver's license, was dependent on the public transit system in Louisville. One day, when his bus failed to show up on time, Clinton became fearful he'd be late for work. So he walked there. But Clinton only knew one way to get to work on his own and that was to take the same route that the bus did. So, walking miles out of his way, Clinton did just that. He walked the bus route.

It is that dedication to do a good job that speaks so eloquently about the desire of people with disabilities to be a part of the mainstream of American life. Today, that includes having a job.

The significance of these stories should touch us all for another reason. There is not one of us exempt from the possibility of joining the group described in sixty journal entries here. One arbitrary moment, one misaligned gene can define a lifetime. That, too, is reflected in these pages—in the story of a young woman who was declared dead following a horrific auto accident in Florida and who, today, is reaching new personal goals through her job with the Navy.

The people in these pages cannot be ignored. They reflect absolute truth.

The Javits-Wagner-O'Day Program is the story of the importance of work in the lives of these individuals, their friends and loved ones.

People who see things with their hands.

People who are wonder-full and wunderkinds.

People who must write down certain basic truths at the beginning of each day in order to get through it.

Commitment is the distance that these individuals must run to prove themselves.

These are firebrands, fomenters and malcontents.

Savants, pundits and sages.

People who see every day as the blank canvas that it is and who endeavor to paint it with bold, fearless strokes.

People working in the narrow parameters of routine tasks accomplished in extraordinary ways.

They are the threads that bind the fabric of our country today.

This is America, working.

Introduction

The Javits-Wagner-O'Day Program had its beginnings in 1938. At that time, in our country, many people with disabilities were not working. Those who were working found employment in menial tasks. Some were forced to stand on street corners and beg. The purpose of this legislation was simply to provide work opportunities for people with disabilities and to provide for this from a chunk of the federal procurement dollar—not with appropriated funds. In simple terms, money already spent by government for the purchase of services and products would now be invested in public good. The idea was almost too simple to work. But work it has.

Today, the JWOD Program employs over 30,000 individuals who are blind or severely disabled through the provision of hundreds of services and products to the federal government. It serves as a proving ground for these people to learn life and job skills. For some it means a chance to take these skills and move on to other more difficult work experiences. During the last decade, thousands of people have moved from their jobs on JWOD projects to jobs with other employers in the community.

Sixty years ago, people with disabilities worked by selling brooms and mops on the open market and newspapers and candies in the lobbies of federal buildings. In 1998, people with severe disabilities are working in data entry, recycling, patient escort, switchboard, and other positions. They are working at Presidential libraries, NASA space centers, West Point and the Air Force Academy. They are performing subcontract work for Nissan, General Motors, 3M, Toyota, Mattel, and Boeing. They are working in every state of the union including Alaska and Hawaii.

The JWOD Program is the epitome of social entrepreneurialism. Long before the Vice President's National Performance Review, JWOD was established as a blueprint for government at its best. It takes less than one half of one percent of the federal procurement dollar and invests it in buying services and products from organizations employing people who are blind and severely disabled. In doing so, JWOD provides the best value that government can buy—a service or product at a fair market price, delivered on-time, and at high quality. Moreover, by expanding job opportunities for people with severe disabilities, it assists in putting these individuals to work—lessening or eliminating their need for entitlement programs. At the same time, it brings that individual disposable income and an opportunity for health and welfare benefits too. The end result means economic benefits to the employee and the country too.

In 1996, one JWOD partner, the Occupational Training Center in New Jersey performed a study which illustrated these savings in detail. The end result of that study was that $1.8 million was returned to the economy through the JWOD Program from this one rehabilitation program alone. There are hundreds of such nonprofit community rehabilitation programs and JWOD projects nationwide.

The partnership of two nonprofit organizations and one small federal agency has spelled success for the JWOD Program and the people served by it. National Industries for the Blind, NISH and the President's Committee for Purchase from People who are Blind or Severely Disabled work together to provide assistance and direction. The community rehabilitation programs provide the additional training and support services necessary for the success of the program.

Today, even with the passage of the Americans with Disabilities Act in 1990, estimates of unemployment for people with severe disabilities remain as high as 70%. Waiting lists for JWOD jobs at some facilities are in the hundreds, but thirty thousand other Americans with severe disabilities have found work and are finding success each day through the Javits-Wagner-O'Day Program.

AMERICA, WORKING.

Book and Photographs by Linda Sullivan Schulte

BRYAN BALDWIN

SAN ANTONIO, TEXAS

Bryan Baldwin, 35, works as a computer trainer at the San Antonio Lighthouse for the Blind. Blind since birth due to malformed optic nerves, Bryan teaches computer skills to others who are blind.

Following high school, Baldwin first found work in a plant nursery. Six years later, he was still making minimum wage and he had no benefits. He was married and he was ready to start a family but he needed a higher paying job and more benefits to support that dream.

In 1985, he applied for a position at the Lighthouse and was hired almost on the spot. He has progressed from general assembler to machine operator to quality assurance lab technician and finally to his current position as computer trainer.

While he was working as a lab technician, Bryan used computers to evaluate and document his test results. He discovered that software programs could make many of his tasks easier. He bought a computer for home and through many days and nights taught himself a variety of programs. Encouraged by his supervisor, he applied for the position of computer trainer when it became available. He won it hands down.

The job at the Lighthouse has enabled Bryan to leave the reliance on the Social Security program. He now has the satisfaction of helping others on the same path to independence. He returned to college for further study, is active in his church and spends most of his free time with his daughters. He has become a single parent.

He seldom talks about his disability unless, of course, you watch him at work every day. His actions and commitment to help others speaks volumes.

3

CALVIN BASS

NORFOLK, VIRGINIA

Calvin Bass has been a part of the Eggleston Center since 1969 when he was seventeen years old. He's a Norfolk native with a "whole lot of family" living in the area. He has one brother and two sisters and Calvin lives at home with his parents. With a diagnosis of mental retardation (an IQ of 26) a psychological evaluation determined that Calvin was "unemployable." He began a series of life skills—learning such things as street crossing and calling his supervisor when he was going to be absent.

In 1986, Calvin's attendance in the work environment was reduced due to a diagnosis of sleep apnea. Due to this disorder, Calvin wasn't getting enough sleep at night and as a result, would fall asleep whenever he sat idle for any amount of time. Calvin will typically stop breathing up to 430 times each night.

In 1992, Calvin returned to full-time employment despite his sleep apnea. He accepted a position with the JWOD laundry services contract with Portsmouth Naval Hospital. The hope was that the regular schedule and demanding work flow would help Calvin remain awake and alert throughout the day. Six years later, he remains on the job. His supervisor reports that Calvin understands the importance of his job and its effect on his co-workers. He rarely misses a day with the exception of a family vacation or illness.

Calvin's mother believes that his job at the JWOD site has meant a great deal to him. Despite the sleep apnea, which sometimes leaves him very tired, he is always up at 7 a.m. and ready for work. Calvin is proud of the uniform he wears everyday and he's especially proud of his new photo I.D. badge which he wears to work each day. On the few days that he's forgotten the badge, he's insisted he return home to get it.

Calvin has become more independent in his personal life too. Mrs. Bass takes Calvin to the grocery store weekly where he selects and pays for his lunch items. Receiving his pay check in the mail is something he looks forward to as well. He uses his earnings to buy his own clothes, shoes and more.

When the Eggleston Services team participated in a corporate trip to Busch Gardens in Williamsburg, Virginia, Calvin utilized payroll deductions to buy tickets for himself, mother, father and his nephew. Part of his earnings has gone to buy a special adjustable bed which is helping with his sleep disorder.

He's been named Employee of the Year at the Center. "I really like my job. I like to fold sheets, put pillowcases in the machine. I like to come to work on time because I don't want to be late. I like to sweat."

Calvin's work in the laundry confirms that he is a contributing member of a team providing services to the Portsmouth Naval Hospital.

THOMAS BRENNEN

PITTSBURGH, PENNSYLVANIA

The smile that is almost always on Tommy Brennen's face belies the many years of difficulties and challenges that he has weathered throughout his life. Diagnosed with spina bifida, Tommy first came to the Easter Seal Society of Western Pennsylvania through its pre-school program in Pittsburgh, Pennsylvania.

Tommy's physical condition makes it necessary for him to wear a heavy brace which runs almost the full length of his body and virtually prohibits his ability to turn and move. This, coupled with the fact that he uses a wheelchair, makes competitive employment in his community an illusive goal.

After graduating through the special education program, and a short stint with the CETA (Comprehensive Employment and Training Act) Program, the staff of the Office of Vocational Rehabilitation referred Tommy to the Easter Seal Society of Western Pennsylvania for employment. There, the folks at Easter Seals helped to modify a job station for Tommy's particular needs and to help him in his position as kit assembler. Working on the production line for the Pocket Planner (used by countless government employees worldwide), Tommy helps to assemble the reams of pages that make up the mini-appointment book. He worked at this job until March of 1993 when he was transferred to the Time Management Department to work as a Desk Pad Assembler and Machine Operator. In this department, Tommy's job requires great manual dexterity and a high degree of attention to detail —two attributes which are strengths for Tommy.

Proud of his work at ESSWP, and armed with the confidence and independence he has gained, Tommy recently realized his long-time goal of moving into his own apartment. He also rides the city's accessible transportation system to work every day. His attendance on the job is almost perfect despite the fact that he lives quite a distance from the facility.

Tom recently began to pursue his goal of moving on to community employment away from the Javits-Wagner-O'Day Program. He has attended a local job fair geared for individuals with disabilities and got several job leads. With the skills and experience that he's learned at Easter Seals, Tom should excel at any job he chooses.

STEVEN BROWN

SOMERSET, NEW JERSEY

Steven Brown knew he wanted to work, knew he could work from an early age. The difficulty was in convincing everyone else that he could. With vision, hearing and cognitive disabilities from an early bout with rubella, Steven was faced with a work world that was inflexible and resistent to give him a chance.

So, for many years, Steven lived in an institution run by the state. He also attended a variety of specialized schools including the Helen Keller National Center for Deaf/Blind Youths and Adults in New York. There, he learned American Sign language and other daily living skills.

Almost five years ago, the New Jersey Association for the Deaf/Blind (NJADB) started an industrial program and it became a lynchpin for Steven's desire for work. He is a steady and dependable worker.

His steady employment has given Steven the opportunity to move into a group home. Every morning he wakes up and asks if it is a work day. "I like my friends at work. I like to talk to people and I like a chance to make money," he says. Steven works on tasks including packaging, collating, sorting and light assembly work. He refuses to take a break until all of the work on his table has been completed.

9

MICHAEL CAMPBELL

PITTSBURG, KANSAS

To hear Michael Campbell talk, his insight on life has actually been accentuated by the physical limitations that his body's endured throughout the years.

He was diagnosed with diabetes when he was six. He received his first laser treatments for diabetic retinopathy at age 18. Michael worked at various jobs after graduating from high school but diabetes ended his primary dream which was to enter the military. He married and started a family. His work experiences were constantly in flux as each further erosion of his eyesight would rob him of job after job. "My eyes would go out and I would have to quit my job, and look for another one." Michael would be forced to start all over at the bottom rung of another job. He would get to the point where he would be making "good money" and then he'd be faced with another challenge and "it got harder and harder to make ends meet" in the San Diego area.

When he was told that laser treatments could no longer be continued, Michael moved his wife and their two daughters to Pittsburg, Kansas, in order to be near other family members. He spent the next 10 years at home and took some classes at Pittsburg State University with the goal of obtaining a business degree. Again, complications arose from his diabetes and one of his legs was amputated.

In 1993, he contacted a rehabilitation center and was told about employment opportunities at a new manufacturing facility at the Wichita Industries and Services for the Blind. He was one of the first people to interview for a position there and has worked there ever since. Over the years, he's performed jobs such as machine operator, box erector, and presently shrink-wrap operator.

In 1994, Michael's other leg developed an infection and it too, was removed. His job at WISB has enabled him to support his family and his wife who often babysits their grandaughter. "I know that even if my eyes go out totally, I'll still be able to support my family—and that's a great feeling."

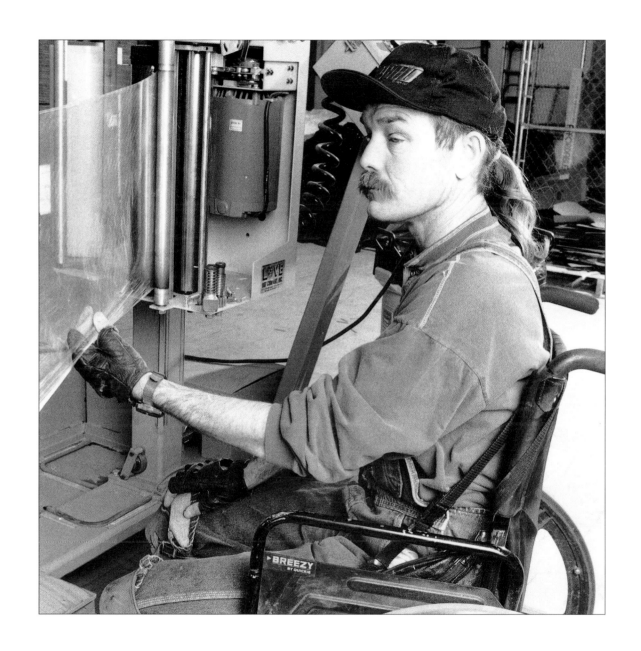

SHIRLEY CLARK
WICHITA FALLS, TEXAS

Eighteen years ago, Shirley Clark arrived on the scene at the Work Services Corporation in Wichita Falls, Texas, and began her career. At 44 years of age, Shirley had found herself with a body that cerebral palsy had made almost impossible for her to control. Simple mechanical efforts became—extraordinary feats for her. With poor motor skills and a severe speech impairment, Shirley faced a bleak employment outlook. She had, in fact, been unable to work successfully in a variety of positions in the local community.

But this wife of a retired Navy man and mother of two children was determined to win employment and help support her family. With the help of WSC and the Javits-Wagner-O'Day Program, that's exactly what she has done.

Armed with a sharp mind, the tremendous support of her co-workers at WSC and the stability of a JWOD project under which over 1,000,000 paper clips are manufactured each day, Shirley has achieved the goal of employment. First, she excelled as a quality control inspector and today, she serves as a Production Lead Worker for the community rehabilitation program.

According to her supervisor, "The single reason that she cannot find other employment is a physical disability that is beyond her control. Yet, she tries to continue to improve daily in both her motor and communicative skills." Shirley is completely dedicated to producing quality products.

Shirley has one grandchild and says that her most relaxing hobby is sewing. She has one other passion besides working and that is support for "her" Dallas Cowboys.

TIM COCKERHAM

Las Cruces, New Mexico

It was always hard to catch up with Tim Cockerham in the dining hall facility at the White Sands Missile Range. Working as a mess attendant, Tim attacked his job much like he attacks life - head on and with total abandon. Taken in at the age of four and a half by foster parents Naomi and Albert Grady, Tim faced numerous challenges. He couldn't walk. He couldn't talk. In addition to Down Syndrome, he was lagging behind many children his age in physical development. To many people, he seemed more like a two-year-old than almost five. After testing, Tim was deemed to have the aptitude of a two-month-old. His physical limitation demanded that he use a walker to get around. Early on, while trying to manipulate his walker he fell and broke his leg—resulting in one leg becoming shorter than the other. But if any one thought that these conditions would slow Tim Cockerham down, they were proven wrong. With every obstacle presented to him, Tim seemed to just get stronger and more determined. The Gradys, whose own children were older, provided the time and a support system for Tim that was unparalleled. He flourished with care. After completing high school, Tim was placed on a waiting list for a job, but jobs in Las Cruces are hard to come by. For two years, Tim stayed at home with his parents until Tresco, Inc., a community rehabilitation program, called him to work on a Javits-Wagner-O'Day Program. At the dining hall facility, Tim's primary responsibilities were dishwashing, cleaning tables, and assisting in food preparation. He liked to be busy and was happiest during the lunch hour rush when his workload was heaviest. Tim's dependability speaks for itself—his attendance record there was over 95% for his three years on the job. His productivity level rose from 75% to 100% on the job. In December of 1995, Tim was chosen White Sands Disabled Employee of the Year. In 1997, the White Sands Facility was closed—part of the BRAC initiatives. Although Tim was disappointed, he again jumped right into new work at the Fort Bliss/ McGregor Dining Facility. Then, another hurdle— this project ended and Tim was, again, unemployed through situations outside his control. Referred back to his rehabilitation team at Tresco, Inc., Tim works today on a crew responsible for custodial and grounds maintenance work in the Las Cruces area. He is a shining example of the employment possibilities for individuals who have the determination and opportunity to succeed.

GLORIA COLON

SHREVEPORT, LOUISIANA

When Gloria Colon's mother died in 1977, it marked a pivotal moment for Gloria. She was faced with chronic depression—formally diagnosed as depressive neurosis and schizoid personality—and, as a result, was facing a life that was losing all definition and balance. Despite having a degree from Centenary College in Shreveport, Gloria was unable to cope with virtually any stress and could not keep a job.

As a result, Gloria was referred to North Louisiana Goodwill Industries in March of 1991 for job training. Although her attitude and desire to succeed were very commendable, this effort was largely unsuccessful because of low self-confidence and lower productivity. Despite this initial experience, Gloria expressed a positive desire to work with Goodwill in seeking competitive employment through the job placement program.

Not too long after, Goodwill received a JWOD contract to provide shelf stocking services at the near-by Barksdale Air Force Base Commissary. Since everyone on the Goodwill staff had been impressed by Gloria's tenacity and desire to succeed, she was hired as a day stocker in October of 1993. Since that day, there's been a remakable reversal in Gloria's life. It is abundantly evident to everyone around her that her positive traits finally dominate her life again. She has a strong desire to perform quality work and is sensitive to the needs of commissary customers. Gloria projects genuine pride in her job, herself, and the joy she has in serving others. The Commissary Officer stated in a recent letter of appreciation to Goodwill that "Gloria's professionalism and dedication to serving customers is outstanding." What isn't mentioned is that Gloria is coping now with the stresses associated in providing these services in a busy commissary environment.

As a result of her success in the workplace, Gloria now serves on the Board of Directors of NISH and is helping define policy and programs to serve other people with severe disabilities nationwide.

CHRISTINE COOK
FT. WORTH, TEXAS

Christine Cook is a pioneer of sorts. She is presently employed in a unique Javits-Wagner-O'Day Program which provides temporary administrative services to the federal government. Spurred on by reinventing, downsizing and contracting out initiatives, the General Services Administration in Fort Worth, Texas, found itself in need of more administrative muscle. Facing severe budget restrictions, they sought temporary relief by employing people with disabilities through JWOD to do the work. Christine was one of the first to sign on—referred by the Texas Commission for the Blind.

The opportunity gave the single mother the chance to get "off welfare" where she had been receiving food stamps and medicaid to help support herself and her two young sons. Legally blind from Retinitis Pigmentosa, a degenerative eye condition, Christine was first assigned secretarial work on a temporary services project in Dallas. Excelling there, she jumped at the chance to work in her hometown of Fort Worth when her present position became available. Christine's job is to inventory and library the thousands of purchase orders that GSA maintains.

The job has taught Christine a number of things, improved her job skills and allowed her the economic freedom to pursue a degree as a legal assistant - a career that would have been virtually impossible a few short years ago. But the thing that Christine says she has gained the most from the job at GSA doesn't cost anything. "It's given me self-esteem."

MYRTLE COOK

AIKEN, SOUTH CAROLINA

Everyone says the same thing about Myrtle Mae Cook—she's goal oriented. If she weren't so dedicated and focused, chances are her life would have been quite different.

According to old State records, she was born in 1945 and her father was "unknown." Her family lived in a quagmire of poverty and ignorance. Her house was filthy. She and her brothers and sisters lived on the floor. Her clothing was inadequate and none of the children had shoes. At the age of 14, Myrtle was adopted by a local couple—but, unfortunately, this ended in disaster too. Social workers removed her from the situation and in 1971, Myrtle was placed in an institutional setting. At that time, one worker wrote: "Her retardation is obvious, and her potential is quite undetermined."

That potential began to be better defined when she was referred to Tri-Development Center in 1987. For the first three years there, Myrtle was responsible for a variety of jobs including assembly work, sorting, food preparation and custodial tasks. In 1991, she demonstrated such promise that she moved to community-based environment on a mobile custodial crew. Later that year, Myrtle asked for assignment to a JWOD project at a nearby Army Reserve Center.

She stayed there for 15 months and capitalizing on her rave reviews there—and the life and work skills taught to her by TDC—Myrtle became a candidate ripe for employment in the community. She was hired first by the Market Street Buffet and Bakery and then transferred to Burger King (a division of the same company).

Myrtle was recognized for her work in 1996 when she was selected to receive the Evelyne Villines Award for outstanding work following her participation on a JWOD Project. Since that time, she and her husband purchased a home, accomplishing another one of her dreams. She recently underwent surgery but is looking forward to re-entering the world of work in the near future. She remains as determined as ever to live the independent life that she has labored so hard to achieve. Her smile and laughter continue to brighten the lives of her many friends throughout her community.

Employment and determination have carried Myrtle a long way. Today, she is married and a home-owner. Before going to bed each night, Myrtle kisses her husband, Carl, and her dog, Lady, goodnight and covers the cages of her four pet cockatiels.

MARK DODD

FT. WORTH, TEXAS

Mark navigates his way around the high-rise office in the General Services Administration building in downtown Fort Worth as though he were on automatic pilot. To watch him in this environment, working feverishly at his computer, you would never realize that he's blind. The first clue might be the voice synthesizer of his computer terminal itself. Mark feels that "blindness has never been a problem for me personally ... ever." His parents instilled him with a strong work ethic and a determination to excel at anything he chose to pursue.

Before coming to the GSA temporary services project, Mark taught at a nearby community rehabilitation program called Expanco. His primary job there was teaching people with disabilities about computers. But he wanted employment in the community—on his own.

"My view is that I don't know what my limitations really are because I keep pushing them to see how far I can go. I've never accepted that what I'm doing today is what I'll be doing for the rest of my life." His work at GSA proves this. When he was assigned a particular task as part of his job, he found that there was no software that would allow him to do that task. So what did Mark do? He simply programmed one himself, complete with graphics, which would do the job. It took countless hours and working at home to succeed, but Mark prevailed.

"My feeling is that when an employer is willing to give me a chance to show what I can do they are going to get my best," Mark says "And there are so many others with disabilities that have never had that opportunity who would provide an employer with a dedicated and loyal employee if just given that chance."

23

JENNIFER EICKHOFF

St Paul, Minnesota

Cerebral palsy, mental retardation, hearing loss and impaired speech would be challenges for any four people, but one individual with all of these disabilities—Jennifer Eickhoff—has overcome these and, along the way, established a successful career.

One of five children, Jenny, with the support of her strong and caring family and a rehabilitation team at Minnesota Diversified Industries (MDI), succeeded in her goal of achieving independence through positive employment.

Jenny has been doing exemplary work at Minnesota Diversified for 15 years. Currently, she is working in the MDI Government Services Department as a packager/assembler. She works four hours a day assembling stamp products as part of a contract with the U. S. Postal Service. Always ready to try new tasks, Jenny plays an active role at MDI as she represents herself and her co-workers as a member of the company's advisory committee. An important team player, she attends and volunteers for various other MDI functions too.

In addition to her job responsibilities at MDI, Jenny has worked at various community-based settings too. This reflects Jenny's work ethic and her desire to succeed in any employment setting. Jenny says that she enjoys her job and hopes to continue to do it well.

For fun, Jenny enjoys taking vacations with her parents. She has lived in her own apartment for many years, but admits that sometimes it's tough having a roommate.

When Jennifer was asked to describe her favorite part of working at MDI, she replied: "friends."

TIMOTHY FESTER

DOVER, DELAWARE

Tim Fester is one of three sons with developmental disabilities born to Margaret and Robert Fester. The two oldest sons, William and Robert, had lesser degrees of difficulties but Tim, it seemed, would be the biggest challenge. In addition to his learning disabilities, he was born with a cleft pallet and had great difficulty communicating. Margaret talks about a comment made to them three decades ago about the future for Tim. "They told us, with all of his problems, Tim should be put in a home." But the Festers believed that "there was always a chance for growth for him and we've been proven right."

The Festers had been living in Biloxi, Mississippi, but knew that Dover, Delaware, offered more hope for Tim in terms of employment and training possibilities. So in 1989, they moved there. Working with Kent-Sussex Industries and The Chimes, Tim has received both the training and the opportunities he required. It wasn't easy. Crowds of people would absolutely terrorize Tim. He wasn't very secure or confident in what he did.

Today, he works as part of the Javits-Wagner-O'Day Project at Dover Air Force Base. His self-esteem has risen tremendously and he feels good about his work. "Of course," says Mrs. Fester "He loves that paycheck!" He has learned how to sign but hates to use it, so often he'll draw something to help him explain. Recently, efforts have been made to obtain a computerized machine to help him communicate better with his colleagues in the workplace.

He belongs to Wesley Outreach—a group of people with disabilities who get together for recreational events and special trips. He's active in the Special Olympics and in 1995 was a member of the bowling team that participated in the World Games. He loves classical music and can play the organ. Most of all, his mother says, "Tim loves to work. Anything you give him, he'll do to the best of his ability. It may take him time, but once he gets it, and he gets the routine, that's it."

DWAYNE FUGATE

CORBIN, KENTUCKY

Growing up in the small coal mining town of Arjay, Kentucky, offered limited opportunities for young Dwayne Fugate. As a result, he had two primary goals in his life—to graduate from high school and to find an occupation outside of the mining industry. Dwayne graduated from Bell County High School in 1986 and with his diploma in hand, he began his job search. Over the next three-year period, Dwayne worked as a mechanic, a welder and a laborer.

In the late fall of 1988, Dwayne finally accepted the inevitable—a job with a local mining company. A few weeks after reporting to work at the mine, Dwayne was assigned to a maintenance crew to remove specialty equipment from one location to another. Having been told that the power source was disconnected, his supervisor instructed Dwayne to cut the power cables leading to the equipment. An instant later, over 8,000 volts of electricity entered his left arm and exited through his right leg. Medical teams were able to save his leg, but his left arm was amputated. In spite of the severity of the accident, Dwayne refused to accept that his life would be any different from what it had been.

Over the next few months, Dwayne would survive three more accidents that threatened his life. While working on his car, a battery exploded in his face. An automobile accident threw him through the windshield and, a few weeks after that, an accident on an all-terrain vehicle put Dwayne back in the hospital with a severe head injury.

In 1994, Dwayne was referred to Southeastern Kentucky Rehabilitation Industries. He received training while the community rehabilitation facility worked to place him in a job. It was an unsuccessful effort. Months of job interviews and rejections left Dwayne with the clear impression that discrimination against people with disabilities was a stark reality.

Finally, in 1996, a JWOD job as a quality assurance worker opened up. Dwayne grabbed it and within a few months, he was promoted to line supervisor. Today, Dwayne has taken charge of the production of all four of the JWOD projects and over 70 employees. His determination, work ethic, ability to work with people have paid off for Dwayne. He's 29 years old, married with two children, Jacob and Joshua.

29

MARIE-TERESE HENDERSON

ORLANDO, FLORIDA

When police detectives arrived on the scene of a car accident six years ago, they thought at first that there was no need for an ambulance. They were stunned to discover that Marie-Terese Henderson was alive. The car in which she was a passenger had slammed into a pickup truck, flipped on its side, and slid down the shoulder of the road. She had suffered multiple trauma and fractures, compounded by a severe head injury. When she gained consciousness in the hospital, everything that she had taken for granted—breathing, swallowing, talking and walking—all had to be relearned. She couldn't even roll over in bed on her own.

Today, Marie-Terese still stuns people—but for all the right reasons. She is a gentle, vibrant woman who spends many nights after work exercising in the gym. She lives independently in a house that she owns and maintains. She speaks with a voice of inner serenity, camouflaging the mental strength that fueled her to regain all of those skills that she (and others) thought were gone forever. Says Marie "I thought I would never ... participate positively in society after my accident."

For the past two years, Marie-Terese has worked as a supply technician, with government security clearance no less, at the Naval Air Warfare Center in Orlando. She works alongside 1,500 civilian and military personnel there. She still has double vision, bouts with her equilibrium, virtually no short-term memory and occasional episodes of depression. But she has learned to adapt her work to counter these difficulties. Her steno pad is her compass - reminding her each day what duties her job entails. Without these notes, every Monday would seem like the first day on a new job.

Her job is an important one. She controls a fleet of government vehicles, maintains and processes invoices for shipping, assigns priority for printing requests, and manages maintenance and service contracts. Because of her exceptional abilities and strong character, she is a model employee. She has made suggestions that have boosted workplace morale, demonstrates excellent customer services skills and has remained a determined advocate for herself and others who have disabilities.

She attributes much of her success to her family. With their support, she enrolled in college within a year of her accident. She earned an Associates Degree in business skills and graduated with honors, having achieved a 3.85 grade average.

ROBERT HERSHEY

MARIETTA, GEORGIA

One day in November of 1992, while Robert Hershey stood in the middle of the living room of his home, a sound of a thousand freight trains passed near his house. While his brother, Tom, grabbed Robert and forced him to lay down on the floor, a tornado leveled the two neighboring homes and ripped the roof and back from Robert's own house.

With their house uninhabitable, the family was forced to relocate to a nearby hotel. With only one car left that was operable, Robert's sister-in-law Bella, was forced to serve as the family taxi driver, transporting both husband Tom and Robert to work daily. It took months to complete the rebuilding of their home.

Yet, while the experience was traumatic to Robert and the Hershey clan, Robert never missed a day of work as a result of the tornado. "In fact," says Robert's supervisor, "It was weeks later until I even knew that his home had been one of those destroyed by the tornado."

In the face of that scenario, to say that Robert Hershey has a strong work ethic is a gross understatement.

At the age of 66, Robert has faced and overcome a variety of barriers to employment in his lifetime. Back home in West Virginia, his mother had sought for years to shelter Robert from the rest of the world —a philosophy and behavior patterned after that era more than a commitment to rehabilitation. In addition to developmental disabilities, he experienced a variety of health problems, including severe arthritis, a stroke, reduced vision in his right eye and frequent hospitalization and surgery for a chronic back/neck problem.

When Robert's mother needed long-term care in a nursing home, and Robert moved in with his brother and sister-in-law in Georgia, his life began to change dramatically. When Robert became involved with the community rehabilitation program at Tommy Nobis Center in 1986 he couldn't even write his name. He began employment at the Defense Contract Management Command in Atlanta in June of 1987. He proved to be a flexible and cooperative employee working hard to both increase his productivity and improve the quality of his work. His dependability was legend. It wasn't long before he learned to legibly sign his name too—a feat he enjoyed when he endorsed his paycheck.

He experienced a few setbacks along the way during his nine years on the JWOD project but he always overcame them. Health and transportation issues often presented challenges to Robert. Not to mention that tornado.

In September of 1996, Robert retired. A party was given for him to celebrate his entry into the more leisurely pace of life which he had earned and which he enjoyed—until recently.

Reports are that Robert is bored with retirement and wishes to return to a new job.

SAM HOEKSTRA

LAS VEGAS, NEVADA

Sam Hoekstra has been an employee of Opportunity Village (OV) in Las Vegas, Nevada, for over a decade. Today, he works as a commissary shelfstocker on the Javits-Wagner-O'Day (JWOD) project at Nellis Air Force Base Commissary. All of his coworkers call Sam an excellent worker and "one of the nicest people" they know.

It wasn't always that way though.

When Sam first came to Opportunity Village, he was shy, non-communicative and required a great deal of supervision. He was only able to concentrate on one single task at a time and he was assigned to the night shift. Over the years, through the energies of his supervisors and supporters at OV, he has become more outgoing, and he's learned to perform multiple tasks. In addition, Sam needed to develop everyday living skills—like how to dress for work, how to make individual choices, and which social behavior was appropriate in certain situations. He was promoted to the day shift because his appearance improved as well as his ability to work independently. In 1995, he was voted by his supervisors and peers to be employee of the month—a big step for Sam away from his troubled past.

Sam participates in the Special Olympics as a basketball player and his teammates praise both his ability and his team spirit.

Through his employment at Nellis AFB, Sam helped contribute a portion of his earnings so that he and his mother were able to purchase a home together.

SANDRA HOLLAND

ROCKVILLE, MARYLAND

The Vocational Services Division of the Arc of Montgomery County, Maryland, began its first JWOD contract at the Department of Energy's Child Development Center in August, 1993. Sandra Holland was one of the first employees to work at the site. As with any new project, the folks at the Arc were concerned about the scope of the undertaking. Sandra, however, was so enthusiastic and determined to make the site successful that her "excitement carried the day." according to her colleagues.

From the very start, Sandra was one of the main public relations resources. She told everyone about her new job and how happy she was to have it. She was excited to work at a child care center even though she would have to miss her Friday night dances. The Department of Energy (DOE) enclave requires evening work. Sandra worked diligently from the start—helping to bring in equipment and supplies for the initial setup. She was on-time every evening—no small task since she had to take public transportation to meet her Job Coach for the last leg of the trip. She displayed nothing short of 100% confidence in her abilities to do the job and soon, she was the backbone of the project. Not only did she perform her job, but she knew everyone else's work

schedule and pitched in with extra duties when others were absent. She knows the complete list of duties for the daily, weekly and monthly schedule. Often, Sandra checked on the Job Coach by asking her if the weekly spray buffing had been done yet.

Sandra's attention to quality of service is outstanding. She may prompt a coworker when something is missed or bring an issue to the attention of the Job Coach. Sandra reports any problems promptly and she is trusted to report problems professionally using the appropriate chain of command with her supervisors—often a challenge for people with mental retardation.

In 1994, through her own request and strong self-advocacy skills, Sandra lobbied for a daytime job that would not take her away from her leisure activities that she loved. After several false starts and not finding one that was the right match, Sandra returned to the DOE in 1996 and has worked there ever since.

Today, Sandra lives with two housemates in an Alternative Living Unit supported by the Arc. She is active in her community and enjoys volunteering with senior citizens. She is a strong self-advocate and she participates in several self-advocacy groups.

37

MARIAN HOLLARS

WICHITA FALLS, TEXAS

On March 3, 1968, Marian Hollars arrived at the Work Services Corporation (WSC) in Wichita Falls, Texas. Her medical and vocational prognosis stated that the facility was the best and only employment setting that Marian could hope for. For the next 28 years, Marian worked at WSC—primarily on a production line manufacturing paper clips for the Javits-Wagner-O'Day Program. Marian's supervisors, her parents, her vocational rehabilitation counselor and the work center staff had concluded that Marian would never work outside WSC.

Marian, however, had other plans. She had watched several of her coworkers (with less severe disabilities) move into employment in the commercial sector and she decided that she wanted to follow in their footsteps. With some reluctance, the folks at WSC agreed to conduct another vocational evaluation to determine Marian's potential for employment outside the facility. The results were predictable. Marian, the report said, lacked the physical stamina, intellectual ability, communicative skills, and emotional stability for successful employment in the community. Again, the JWOD project was recommended as the optimal employment outcome for Marian. But this news still didn't deter her. If anything, it intensified her resolve.

Finally, after months of persistence, Marian was able to convince WSC to find her a job out in the community. In June of 1996, at the age of 46, Marian started working at the Bargain Depot, a retail sales store in Wichita Falls. Initially, Marian's duties were limited to greeting customers and returning shopping carts from the parking lot to the store. Through her own initiative, Marian expanded her duties to include stocking shelves, cleaning up spills, and helping cashiers sack merchandise. The store manager was so impressed with Marian's performance that she decided to add various tasks in the store lunch counter to Marian's daily schedule. Marian passed the Wichita County Health Department Food Handler Test on the first try. As a result, she now fills food orders, cleans counters, tables and trays in addition to her other duties in the store. The store manager reports that: "Marian makes decisions as to the priority of her tasks. She works on her own with very little supervision. She sees what needs to be done and quickly carries it out enthusiastically."

"My regular customers love Marian," says the store manager "and she can greet most of them by name."

Marian contributes monthly to the Children's Home of Abilene, Texas, and to Prison Ministries. On the job at Bargain Depot, she conducts tours for special education students from area high schools. In a recent conversation, Marian recalled how no one thought she could make it in the community. She added: "I showed'em, didn't I?"

39

GERALDA HOOKS

DAYTON, OHIO

In October of 1994, after a long history of health problems, doctors told Geralda Hooks that her kidneys would fail within a year. She began dialysis without much success. The treatments left her weak, lethargic, dizzy and with numbness in her limbs. She had held a job as housekeeper at a local hotel and had to give it up. She was also no longer able to take care of her young son. Months passed and in August of 1995, her name was placed on a donor list for a kidney transplant. Due to the severity of her condition, she received a transplant just two weeks later.

After six months of recuperating and rebuilding her strength, Geralda began to look for a job. The job search was frustrating and tiring because few employers wanted to risk hiring someone who had just had a kidney transplant. Health insurance was an issue too. "Everyone thought I was going to die," Geralda says today. Determined to work, she came to Goodwill Industries of the Miami Valley. She went to work on a part-time basis on a Javits-Wagner-O'Day project at Wright-Patterson Air Force Base where she received continuing case management and counseling services.

Work was hard for her there at first. She resisted the training—after all, she'd worked as a housekeeper before and felt her experience had given her all of the insight she needed. But soon, Geralda learned about the quality required on a JWOD project. She became more thorough and more fixed on inspecting her own work. She did such a good job in fact, that she was promoted to a team leader position where she trained other people with disabilities. "It was exciting for me..." she says today.

In 1997, Geralda was hired as supervisor on a new custodial project at the Twin Valley Psychiatric System. As a result of the quality she demonstrates in her work there, Goodwill was recently asked to expand the services on Geralda's contract—including adding another shift. This will mean more jobs for other people with disabilities.

WAN RONG HUANG

SAN FRANCISCO, CALIFORNIA

The first thing you notice about Wan is her smile. The second thing you get to see is the photo of her son in cap and gown.

Wan has been an employee on the custodial services project at the Philip Burton Federal Building in downtown San Francisco for over six years. Her full-time work there has helped her son achieve his dream of attending college .

Wan was placed through the California Department of Rehabilitation with the community rehabilitation program, Toolworks, in San Francisco. She had been born deaf and raised in a rural area of China during the revolution. She had no education and was "looked down on" by her countrymen. She worked as a laborer with "no rights" in her native land. She married a man who was also deaf and then, together, they had a son who was deaf. It was at that time they decided that their dreams for their son would only become reality in the United States. They emigrated to the United States and built the new life they had sought there. She and her husband both found employment on a JWOD contract through Toolworks. More than just a job, the work there has changed their lives, made a home possible and allowed their son to attend the University of California. Says Wan: "I am able to give my son a good education."

Wan is a very independent worker despite having to learn various languages. Not only didn't she know English but she didn't know any sign language either. Today, fluent in the American Sign Language, she says: "I was quiet when I first came here, now I am happy, friendly and outgoing."

HEATHER HUGHES
WICHITA FALLS, TEXAS

Her hands are a blur when she talks and she talks fast too. All of her words pouring out in a kind of continuous run-on sentence. In fact, every action that Heather Hughes undertakes seems to be at top speed. She is a blur of motion when she busses tables at her job as mess attendant at Sheppard Air Force Base too. This is important because she alone is responsible for bussing and cleaning 350 tables in a span of time from 10:30 a.m. until 1 p.m. every day. Picking up the utensils, dishes and leftovers from servicemen and women is important to her. "I love my job. I love the people, my bosses and I have always had a dream of working in the dining hall here." she says smiling. She has an infectious laugh that punctuates every sentence.

During an Air Force inspection, the evaluators specifically recognized Heather as a "Professional Performer" in 1998. Her work has been highlighted on "Sheppard Spectrum" a local basewide cable television program.

Heather's story—not unlike many others—is one of persistence. At 42 years of age, Heather recently moved out of her group home and into an apartment of her own. Even though she has the support of a close, caring and talented family, she did this against the wishes of her parents and even her two brothers. "They didn't like it," she says "but I proved them wrong." The truth is that her family was more protective of Heather and concerned for her vulnerability. At first, Heather wasn't wild about the group home situation. "There was a lot of fussing and fighting." she reports.

Heather graduated from the special education course in Wichita Falls. In her spare time, She likes to watch television, eat and bake cookies. "I'm a good dancer too," she says enthusiastically. She has a crush on a young man named Tommy. One of her brothers is a trumpet player who travels with internationally-known musician Yanni and Heather is looking forward to them coming to perform in Dallas.

BILLY JAMES
SEDALIA, MISSOURI

Employed as a fisheries aide for the Missouri Conservation Department since 1993, Billy James processes fish scales, catfish spines and paddlefish jawbones for age and growth analysis, packages information into Kids Fishing Clinic packets, and assists with willow staking projects on stream banks.

At age three, Billy was diagnosed with mental retardation, coordination problems and autistic tendencies. He attended preschool and therapy classes at the Children's Therapy Center in Sedalia and special education classes in the Sedalia public schools. As a teenager, Billy found his way to Cooperative Workshops, Inc. One of Billy's first job experiences included working on a Javits-Wagner-O'Day project manufacturing metal file boxes for the General Services Administration. When a manager at CWI received a call from the Fisheries District Supervisor describing a job opportunity for a person with a disability, he set up an internal selection process to find the right candidate. Five employees were selected, all of whom had received work experience through JWOD. According to Elveera Satterwhite of CWI, the "skills and discipline learned through JWOD's quality and training processes had equipped each of them for the next step toward advanced employment."Billy James was the candidate hired for the job.

According to his Fisheries supervisor, Billy was selected not only for his capabilities but for "his interest in the job, his eagerness and his good nature." Having worked there now for six years, Billy is a model employee. He's working today on the skills necessary to live on his own—including trying to get his driver's license.

Billy is involved in his community too. He volunteers at the same Children's Therapy Center that he attended years ago and for a self-advocacy group called People to People. He's active in his church and for several years he served on the Board of Directors of NISH, which is the nonprofit organization which helps rehabilitation groups obtain JWOD contracts.

TINA JAMES

BURLINGTON, NEW JERSEY

Some people would say that the odds against Tina James were insurmountably high from the day she was born. Tina was born in Philadelphia, Pennsylvania, and proved to be more than a handful at an early age. She was diagnosed with mild mental retardation and attended a "special studies" school. Tina was eventually moved into a Home for Girls in Erie because she was constantly in trouble. Her uncle took custody of Tina when she found she was pregnant—at age 15. Tina gave birth to a daughter, Diane, shortly thereafter. At age 17, she was living on her own—sharing an apartment with her cousin and collecting welfare and food stamps to survive. One year later, Tina gave birth to Nathaniel (Nate).

Tina then moved back in with her aunt and uncle and a number of other cousins and relatives. She wanted to reduce her hefty rent payment and her aunt had offered her space for $150 a month. It was then—faced with two young children and a strong desire to work—that Tina sought out help. In May of 1997, that help came in the form of job counselors from the Occupational Training Center (OTC) of Burlington County. Tina had been referred by the Department of Vocational Rehabilitation to OTC and the counselors there directed her toward the Javits-Wagner-O'Day food service project at McGuire Air Force Base. The employees at OTC taught her the food service skills needed at McGuire—everything from serving on the line, to bussing tables. to operating the commercial dishwasher. Her wages today are close to $9.00 an hour.

At first, she needed numerous supports. Tina says: "I had a big attitude problem. They'd get bad reports, but I changed a lot..." She credits her OTC counselor for her change of heart, but says, "I had to change for me...not just for the job." Tina also had to change for other reasons. Shortly after Tina took the job at the Air Force Base, she discovered that her young daughter, Diane, was so proud of her mother that she ran through the neighborhood telling everybody that her mother was off welfare.

Today, Tina works five hours a day on the dinner shift and will soon be moving to an earlier shift so she can be there for her children when they come home from school. Her next goal is to get a place of her own and ultimately find a job nearer her home.

48

USHONE JOHNSON

NORTH HIGHLANDS, CALIFORNIA

Three years ago, when Pride Industries officials were looking to find people with disabilities for a JWOD food service project at Travis AFB, California, they visited the Solano County Office of Education to interview three students in the special education course for part-time work. Their hope was to be able to train them and when they graduated with the enhanced work skills, to pursue full-time employment for them. The students had been identified as having a tough time competing for work with students who didn't have disabilities. By the end of the day, the Pride counselor hired one of the students, Ushone Johnson. He started his first job two weeks later. Ushone brought one attribute with him that endeared him to his supervisors—potential. He was as far from work-ready as anyone could get, but he had potential. He required constant supervision and direction. His work lacked quality and he couldn't stay on task. He wandered through the dining facility and was continually mumbling to himself, mostly expletives. He could not remember the simplest of job tasks. He would not open up to anyone and his co-workers stayed away.

Pride officials persevered and so did Ushone. Today, he is able to perform all tasks required of him. He has missed only three days of work since February of 1994. He has a good attitude and is admired and respected by all co-workers and staff. He uses complete sentences when communicating. Ushone has become an excellent role model for all employees with disabilities. He is able to manage public transportation by himself—both to and from work. His mother is still his biggest fan. They are both involved in their Salvation Army Church.

WILLIAM KIMMONS

ALBUQUERQUE, NEW MEXICO

William Kimmons was working for 20 years on a variety of product jobs for a community rehabilitation program called RCI, Inc. in Albuquerque, when he decided it was time to move on. Bill knew that despite his cerebral palsy and hearing loss, he had not been working to the extent of his capabilities. All he needed was the opportunity to demonstrate these capabilities and someone to provide the assistive technology to help him get there. The team at RCI, Inc., focused on what he could do. Bill's strengths included piloting his electric wheelchair and his affection for and ability with mechanical devices.

Bill and his team made several unsuccessful attempts at finding jobs, including disassembling machinery and working at hardware stores. Then a member of the RCI team had an idea: they could adapt a vacuum to fit Bill's chair so he could work on one of RCI's JWOD projects. Bill liked the idea. It combined his abilities with his wheelchair with his desire to operate machinery. With the aid of the Division of Vocational Rehabilitation and staff from the University of New Mexico's Research Institute for Assistive and Training Technologies they obtained the expertise and resources to provide the adaptation. In addition, the staff worked with Bill to obtain a new communication board so he might better express himself. As Bill waited for his adaptation, Bill asked to work at Kirtland Air Force Base so he could prove himself. He began by cleaning water fountains and other fixtures. Once his new vacuum was completely modified, he started his JWOD custodial work and was an instant hit. Bill's success came from his desire to work and succeed in the workplace.

MARY KUGAN

HOT SPRINGS, ARKANSAS

Mary Kugan is the consummate "late bloomer." She came to Abilities Unlimited in Hot Springs, Arkansas, in her mid-forties. Despite this late start in life, she has been hurrying to make up for it ever since. Mary has epilepsy, low vision and mental retardation.

Raised in a series of foster homes, Mary had been virtually locked out of a society by a system which, at that time, tended to lose track of the individual while trying to redeem the collective. When Mary arrived at Abilities, all of that changed. The partnership of Mary's determination and the direction of the skilled team of vocational specialists at Abilities proved to be quite powerful.

Starting slowly, Mary sorted clothes and helped in the kitchen at the Hot Springs facility. She did so well that she was quickly moved to a more demanding job manufacturing and assembling water faucets. Again, she mastered this work and moved on to the custodial project operated under the Javits-Wagner-O'Day Program at the U.S. Post Office Building in downtown Hot Springs.

After being on the JWOD project for only a short time, Mary was selected to be a crew leader and was given more responsibility. She helped with quality control and cost-cutting. She worked every day and would volunteer for overtime as needed.

Thus it was, that this individual, who began with no concept of actually working for pay, nor of living on her own, began to learn the basic skills and ideas necessary for independence. Once she learned them, she mastered them—indeed, she excelled.

By her second year at the Post Office, she was selected for the community rehabilitation facility's Placement Program to seek community employment. Her placement was at a nursing home as a housekeeper. As much as Mary wanted to succeed there, her physical prowess and an extremely demanding employer limited her. Mary fought to accomplish her goals there—she did not want to quit. However, the specialists at Abilities Unlimited made the difficult but necessary decision to remove her.

With a taste of this independence, Mary pressured the folks at Abilities to again find work for her. Within a few months, she was hired by St. Joseph's Hospital as a food service employee in the kitchen. She works there to this day—now working full time. Her title, officially, is "dietary aide." Her job involves preparing the patients' meals and helping to keep the kitchen clean and in good order. "Don't know what we would do without her." says her supervisor, John Showers.

GARY LANGENSTEIN

DOVER, DELAWARE

Gary Langenstein's life seemed to be moving forward with the steady predictability of most Americans. He served six years in the Navy. He got married and had two daughters. Then one morning, he left for work as usual but when he returned home next his life would be changed forever. On that day, while working up high on a job, Gary slipped and "took a quick dive" onto a concrete pad landing head first. Gary broke his neck, suffered a severe brain trauma and doctors suspected that he would never walk again. In one instant, he had become one of the 350,000 people each year who suffer a traumatic brain injury.

Today, however, Gary supervises a JWOD team of 12 custodians at Dover Air Force Base for The Chimes community rehabilitation organization. It took four years for Gary to get through a most difficult rehabilitation program. He needed help with both his physical and emotional welfare. This long effort culminated with his referral as a client to the JWOD Project at Dover AFB. Four months after his referral to Chimes, he was asked to lead one of the custodial teams there.

The biggest challenge for Gary today is "living up to the high standards that the military sets for the cleanliness of its property." The folks at Chimes manage buildings and maintain crews on the site twenty-four hours a day. He feels good about breaking the old stereotypes of people with disabilities. There are a few residual aftershocks of the head injury, but Gary has learned to live with them.

57

POLLY LEDFORD

CHEROKEE, NORTH CAROLINA

Polly Ledford has spent over a half century living in two worlds.

She is a full-blooded Native American—born on the Eastern Band of Cherokee Indian Reservation in Cherokee, North Carolina. She was born a deaf- mute and as an adolescent attended the North Carolina School for the Deaf. While there, she was diagnosed with mental retardation and diabetes. She was raised in a home environment where the Cherokee language was the primary spoken word and thus, absent any training in sign language of any form, Polly was left to communicate to other family members through a kind of ritual pantomime.

Her early years at Vocational Opportunities of Cherokee consisted primarily of recreational, independent living and pre-vocational activities. But it soon became evident that Polly, when given the chance, could be self-supporting. Her real work training then began. She started with small craft assembly work, moved to laundry folding and to developing custodial skills.

In October of 1988, Polly realized her first mainstream employment through a Javits-Wagner-O'Day project at the Federal Building in nearby Bryson City. This job involved a twenty-mile commute daily for Polly—an experience in itself, since she had seldom before left the reservation. Over the years, Polly showed exceptional ability to learn and carry out the work demands required to ensure quality control standards of the job in Bryson City. The job brought to her, and her family, monetary rewards since the pay was significant for the depressed rural environment in which she lived. Her work on the JWOD project paved the way for Polly to enjoy an annual vacation. In addition, she was able to participate in numerous sessions with a speech therapist and signing professional to improve her ability to communicate in both American and Indian Sign Language.

Polly suffered a stroke in August 1995. She's back at the Vocational Opportunities of Cherokee now working on light custodial work and small craft assembly. Her goal is to build herself up to go back to work on another JWOD project. She's fighting daily frustrations with determination to return to her job. She has gone through physical therapy and no longer walks with a cane.

YIM FUTT LEE

LONG ISLAND, NEW YORK

A six-year employee at the Lighthouse Industries in Long Island City, Yim Futt Lee's commitment to excellence and to his fellow coworkers has made his professional and personal life a true success story.

A native of Burma, Yim Lee came to this country to pursue his dream of becoming a chef. At 37, however, he experienced an onset of blindness—the culmination of several medical problems, including a spot on his right eye. He was examined by many specialists, but despite their care, the problems persisted and grew increasingly worse.

During this same period, Yim Lee suffered from a bout with ulcers. The doctor who was treating him for this condition prescribed a medication which caused severe allergic reactions—including fainting spells and bleeding ulcers. Blood transfusions were the only method to alleviate the bleeding ulcers and these, in turn, caused Yim Lee more problems. He lost the sight in both eyes due to toxic optic atrophy.

With the loss of his vision, Yim Lee became depressed and worried about the loss of independence and mobility. He feared he would be unable to support his wife and four children. Encouraged by his family, friends and social workers, Yim Lee sought counseling. In time, he overcame his depression. Referred to the Jewish Guild for the Blind, he spent the next five years learning mobility, independent living and job skills. He wanted desperately to return to work.

Having once worked as a tailor, Yim Lee was encouraged to redevelop those skills. He renewed this skill with great gusto and became so proficient that his counselor suggested that he apply for a job as a sewing machine operator with the Lighthouse. He did so and started working there fulltime in 1987. Today, Yim Lee is into weightlifting, exercise and sports and he spends his free time helping others who have visual impairments. Every summer, Lee and his family attend Visions Camp for the Blind where people interact through recreational activities and support programs. He is active in Chinatown's blind community, holding monthly meetings in which legal and political issues, job accessibility and public education are discussed.

Yim Lee has worked hard to bring success to his family and to himself. Today, he works hard to help his friends find those opportunities too.

61

DIANA LEWIS

CHARLOTTESVILLE, VIRGINIA

As a Certified Nursing Assistant (CNA), Diana Lewis' primary tasks are centered around caring for the elderly residents in a skilled care unit at Westminster Canterbury of the Blue Ridge. She also helps the nursing staff with routine paper work too.

Born with congenital cataracts, Diana underwent several eye operations as a child—which delayed her entry into the school system. But that's all that was delayed. Diana's desire to succeed was not. She attended the Romney School for the Blind in West Virginia and while there, married and had two sons.

In 1986, she moved to Virginia. It was not, however, an easy move. Faced with challenges in her marriage, Diana soon found herself a single parent with two sons and she was forced to find her first employment outside the home. Virginia Industries for the Blind trained and hired her. Through this opportunity, Diana demonstrated her drive to succeed by mastering many sewing operations. Soon, she became an accomplished seamstress. During her employment at VIB, she earned her GED and then trained to become a Certified Nursing Assistant. According to her fellow workers, she's a reliable employee who continually seeks new challenges and responsibilities. Her next goal might possibly be to become a physical therapist.

More than the simple job skills, Virginia Industries and JWOD offered Diana the self confidence that she had been lacking throughout her life. "Without (the Virginia Department for the Visually Handicapped) and my counselor, I doubt that I could have done this." she says "They challenged me and found a way for me to get a job in private industry.

63

DAVID LIZARRAGA

TUCSON, ARIZONA

As a result of a condition attributed to bilateral corneal opacities, David Lizarraga has been blind since he was nine months old. Coupled with his developmental disabilities, opportunities for David seemed limited.

Determined to find a niche for himself, David found a job at the Southwest Contract Connection where he would handle general office work requirements like stuffing envelopes, folding documents and packaging game pieces for a local company. During his work history there, a clinical psychologist had written: " David is not ready for a more competitive work setting...it would be to David's benefit to be in a program where he would be able to develop leisure time and social skills."

Referred to Tempe Center for Habilitation (TCH) by the Tucson Association for the Blind in January of 1995, David began to receive those life skills and enhanced job training as well. Eventually, David was hired as part of the crew at the food service contract at the nearby Air Force Base. He began work as a silverware sorter in the dishwashing room. Impressed with his desire to work and his upbeat personality, David's supervisors moved him to the dining room where he worked the breakfast shift as a busser and stocker. Succeeding there, David was asked to do even more—to help with food preparation by making specialty sandwiches for the lunch meal. He has worked split shifts, extra hours and can be seen working weekends without complaining.

Moreover he is respected by all who have the good fortune to meet him.

David has been selected as Employee of the Month several times and in 1997, TCH named him Employee of the Year.

In his spare time, he volunteers at his local church. David lives with his Mom and Dad and often when he comes home from work, he'll spend time helping his mother in the kitchen. According to his mother, David loves his work so much that he's up and ready for work at five in the morning. His shift doesn't even start until 8 a.m.!

JACK LOWMILLER

WILLIAMSPORT, PENNSYLVANIA

Williamsport, Pennsylvania, is a small rural community known more for its position as the Little League Capital of the World than for employment and industry.

Yet, Jack Lowmiller began his working career there with a small community rehabilitation program named Hope Enterprises. To many citizens there, Jack has become the epitome of excellence in the workplace.

From the beginning, Jack's life was an uphill battle. He was born prematurely and weighed in at a whopping three pounds. His mother was "afraid to carry him home" from the hospital because he was so small and fragile. With a diagnosis of mental retardation and with vision and speech difficulties apparent, Jack attended the public school system as part of a special education curriculum.

Once involved with Hope, Jack began to master work skills on a number of subcontracting jobs—including the woodworking shop there. But he continually sought bigger and more demanding work. In 1984, Jack was selected to be part of a JWOD project at the Federal Building downtown. He did so well there that he was given the additional responsibility of working part-time on another JWOD custodial project at a nearby U.S. Army Reserve Center.

Over the years, Jack has had to assume the additional responsibility of supporting his mother and father with the money he earns from his jobs. He spends very little income on himself and spends a great deal of time supporting his family. He has one dependent—a pet pig he adopted over seven years ago. This gentle man from Hope offers hope to many through his independence and dedication to his work, his community and his family.

MARYANN MACDONALD

Boston, Massachusetts

Maryann MacDonald works for a company which manufactures hot and cold therapy packs for the government. She works with a machine worth thousands of dollars that uses microwaves and tooling to shape the melted vinyl into the desired configuration.

Maryann is in her forties. She's autistic and has severe mental retardation. When these disabilities were first diagnosed, medicine was a lot different. There was little knowledge of the appropriate therapies and rehabilitation techniques. Doctors told Mr. and Mrs. MacDonald that they should just "live with the situation as best (they) could."

When she turned five, Maryann was placed in a day care program.

The teachers were always trying to teach Maryann how to perform even the most basic of tasks, but, they weren't very successful. Maryann could not take care of herself. In fact, her only success in that first day care center was that, at age 6, she learned how to feed herself. Her behavior during that period can only be described as wild. She didn't communicate with anyone. She just seemed to be beyond help.

After five or six years in that program, she ended up at home — sitting and doing nothing. Tutors were sent to try and help, but again, they met with little success. She attended special classes in the local public school.

It some ways, according to her father, it seemed as if Maryann remained a baby—but it wasn't that simple. In addition to her inability to care for herself or to communicate, she exhibited severe behavioral problems with violent temper tantrums. She went from one program to another, and despite all efforts made little real progress. She was eligible for these programs only until she reached the age of 22. So, after 16 years of programs, her parents were back where they started - on their own.

It was at this point that she began a pre-vocational program at Consolidated Products and Services in Massachusetts. She entered the program at the lowest level, and was still exhibiting the same behavioral problems that she had for years. But, with slow deliberation, staff helped Maryann to control her emotions and she began to progress through the vocational program.

She's been employed at CPS, Inc. for 19 years. Before this job, she had few skills and her parents couldn't let her out of the house by herself. She still can't read or write and needs help in certain everyday skills. She has lived for years now in a community residence. Her parents attribute this metamorphosis to her work. According to her father, it put an order in her life that was never there before.

NIC MARSELLO

MISSOULA, MONTANA

From February 1988 until December 1991, Nic Marsello worked on a custodial project at the Federal Building in downtown Missoula, Montana, as part of the JWOD Project. With the help of a community rehabilitation program, Opportunity Resources, Inc. (ORI), he excelled there—demonstrating over and over again his outstanding skills and dedication.

It didn't start out that way however. Nic was armed with a fine work ethic but had few other skills or experience to support employment. He was extremely quiet and reserved. With developing skills, however, came self-confidence. He soon found himself accepted on the crew and he discovered that he could do almost anything put before him. This success fueled his desire to find full-time, long term custodial employment in the community. Nic set his sights on employment at the University of Montana—one of the largest employers in Missoula. When an opening came up, he applied. He was not selected for the position, but supervisors at the University were so impressed with Nic that they converted a work/study position to one specifically for him.

Thrilled about the opportunity, Nic quickly learned that the job demanded flexibility and adjustments. For starters, he was working on the graveyard shift and he needed to adjust his sleep patterns. Nic's determination made the adaptation possible. He continued work on his dream job at the University for five years.

In January of 1997, Nic decided to return to Opportunity Resources to help ORI with the custodial contract at the Aerial Fire Depot. For seven months, he performed outstanding work at that site. In July of that same year, the folks at ORI tapped Nic for work as part of a two-person custodial team at the corporate headquarters. This job demanded individuals who can work independently and perform high quality work. Nic applied and he was hired.

Nic is very proud of the job that he does and feels good about all of the positive feedback the he receives from his co-workers at Opportunity Resources.

PATRICIA MARTINEZ

CLEARFIELD, UTAH

Soon after her birth on St. Patrick's Day, 1965, Patricia Martinez was diagnosed with cerebral palsy. It was apparent that she had other physical difficulties as well—including a hearing loss and resulting speech problems. From that day in March to the present, nothing about Patricia's life has been easy. But through her determination and perseverence, she has often made it look that way. One of her first jobs outside the home was work she found as a custodial employee in the Summer Youth Employment Program in Utah. Following that experience, Patricia came to the Pioneer Adult Rehabilitation Center (PARC) in 1982 as a part-time student. She completed her work adjustment goals and advanced through PARC's Skill Training Program in food service activities. From this experience, she moved to the JWOD parts—sorting project at nearby Hill Air Force Base. With her improving skills, she was given additional responsibilities. Her confidence and pride grew too. And Patricia began to show great interest in helping others with disabilities to be part of the mainstream of the community. PARC then began a custodial contract at the Air Force Base and with Patricia's previous experience, she was given the chance to work there, too.

CHRISTOPHER MAZZA

EAST HARTFORD, CONNECTICUT

In 1995, Christopher Mazza was referred by the State Department of Mental Retardation to the Individual Placement Program at CW Resources in East Hartford, Connecticut.

This referral was no small achievement for Chris. It followed years of institutionalization for him. When he emerged from those facilities, Chris was referred to employment at CW's training center in New Britain, Connecticut, where he first worked as a maintenance person. Coming to grips with a range of personal emotions and adjustments, Chris once showed up for work with a shaved head and shaved eyebrows. His new-found freedom would give flight to his various behaviors. Staff continuously worked with him on life and job skills.

He worked successfully on a Javits-Wagner-O'Day project making and assembling binder clips, and ear plugs.

Over the years at the Center in New Britain, Chris had worked hard to modify his previous behaviors. It was CW's structured work environment, real work for real wages and its expectation of appropriate work behaviors that finally made the difference for him.

As part of his plan, staff recommended that Chris work only one hour per day for just three days a week out in the community. Instead, he was hired to work five hours for five days a week—at a competitive wage. His placement at a McDonalds' cafeteria, located in the Department of Transportation in Newington, has been a success. He has been employed now for several years at McDonalds and has effectively controlled his behaviors enough to maintain the position. Chris does kitchen work and maintenance there. Originally requiring intensive support from the Job Coach, Chris now needs only minimal supervision. He still works five days a week and he recently received a raise. The manager calls Chris "one of (her) most reliable" employees.

Thanks to his work, Chris now lives independently in an apartment supported by the Department of Mental Retardation—a long distance away from the state institution.

LANCESTER McGHEE

WARNER ROBINS, GEORGIA

In 1965, Lancester McGhee was born a happy, healthy baby to loving parents in the small community of Perry, Georgia. At four months of age, he contracted spinal meningitis. The results were severe hearing loss and mental retardation. Yet, through the efforts of his parents and physicians, he began a slow and tedious recovery. He was enrolled in a Speech and Hearing Center and soon was learning to say "Mom" and "Dad." But at the age of four, Lancester was struck by a car. He sustained injuries that required extensive surgery. His vocal cords had been severed. The outlook for Lancester never looked more bleak.

But in spite of his disabilities, Lancester entered the Houston County public school system as part of the special education program. In 1987, at age 21, Lancester McGhee graduated. One year later, he received training in independent living skills. A short time later, he began a job with a furniture store. Unfortunately, this job didn't last long. So he applied for assistance through a local rehabilitation group. He was placed in a job, first at a local restaurant and then, as a maintenance assistant in a large motel. But still, his inability to communicate and his disabilities resulted in his return to the Houston County Association for Exceptional Citizens for more training.

He began anew working in the recycling operations—sorting, baling and working all facets of the operation. When a position became available on the JWOD project at Robins Air Force Base, Lancester jumped at the opportunity. The job involved recycling old tools and parts for the Air Force. He excelled at that job and soon was promoted to another position with the basewide Robins Recycling team. He accompanies the driver as they service about 1,500 housing units picking up recyclables, sorting them at curbside and preparing them for sale.

In his spare time, Lancester participates in virtually all sports associated with the Special Olympics. He bowls on a weekly basis and enjoys dancing too.

TOM MILLER

Tom Miller is a versatile guy. Already at the age of 39, he's been a father, a husband, a member of the Board of Directors of a national nonprofit organization, a dedicated employee, a community activist and more.

Born in West Virginia, Tom graduated from Wirton High School two decades ago. He decided to join his father in South Dakota when he was 30 years old and left the Blue Ridge Mountains behind. Due to his disability, Tom found getting a job almost impossible. He was beginning to get desperate when he interviewed for a job as a groundskeeper with a local business. He was turned down. "I practically begged the man to hire me," Tom says, "I said I would work for a week without pay and I'd prove I could do that job." Again, he was turned away.

A secretary at the company had heard Tom pleading for work, was impressed by both his desire and his dedication and called a friend at rehabilitation services nearby. Soon, Tom was referred to the Black Hills Training Center and was on his way to full-time employment. Today, he works on the JWOD food service contract at the nearby Air Force Base. In addition, he has represented food service employees at a hearing in Washington, DC, and serves on the Board of Directors of NISH.

Understanding the importance of being rescued, Tom recently became a guardian for a dog reprieved from the local shelter—an aging dachshund named "Flash." The dog was so old and infirmed that Tom had to carry him back in his arms every time they went for a walk together. "It's the only dog I could ever catch." he says laughingly.

Tom's biggest source of pride is not his enviable record at work but rather his nineteen-month-old daughter, Tessa, who is clearly the apple of his eye.

His wages earned from his JWOD job make it possible for Tom to raise Tessa as a single parent.

"She is everything to me."

79

CLINTON MONTGOMERY

LOUISVILLE, KENTUCKY

Clinton Montgomery's job in the Javits-Wagner-O'Day Program involved shearing and bending large sheets of metal used in the manufacturing of tool boxes for the government. And Clinton did his job well. Clinton was constantly praised for being a "good, hard worker" and worked diligently to keep up with his coworkers who didn't have a disability.

Raised in an unstable home environment, with a father and sister who had developmental disabilities too, Clinton found himself continuously moved from one institution to another. At one point in his youth, Clinton's capabilities were evaluated and found to be in the category of severe retardation.

In 1971, Clinton came to the community rehabilitation facility known then as Custom Manufacturing Services. There, he began work that many staff people felt would be the most challenging job that

Clinton could handle—sorting mail. Accomplishing one task after another, Clinton worked his way up into the Metal Fabrication Division and into a life of productivity and independence. One of the strongest motivating factors for Clinton is his love of work. On one particularly memorable day, it was discovered that when Clinton happened to miss the bus, he would walk to work. Not knowing the direct route to Custom Manufacturing, Clinton actually walked the route he knew best—the one traveled by the bus each morning—a ten-mile hike.

The confidence that Clinton received from his job has given him the ability to do more with his life. He volunteered with a group called "Dare to Care" in his hometown and today works independently of the JWOD Program.

SONNY MONTGOMERY

DAYTON, OHIO

When I was thirty-five years old, I had a traumatic brain injury, which changed my life," explains Sonny Montgomery at Goodwill Industries of the Miami Valley. At that time, Sonny was involved in an accident in which he was hit on the head by a steel bar. When he awoke in the hospital, even the most basic knowledge eluded him — he was unable to recognize his own family members. He was left with permanent long-term memory loss and short-term memory impairment. It terrified him. He stopped trusting everyone. Sonny's thoughts were not of his wife and children but only of himself. Caught in a wave of depression, he sought solace in alcohol and drugs. He moved out on the streets and only returned home when there were no other options. As Sonny recalls today, for all of this period in his life, he was in a perpetual "fog." He seemed trapped at a dead end.

Thirteen years ago, at the suggestion of a counselor, he came to Goodwill Industries to receive training in custodial services. Sonny still had no memory of what it was like to work much less what it took to succeed in the workplace. He was assigned a job coach to help with the most elementary of tasks. Eventually, he was assigned to the Javits-Wagner-O'Day project at Wright-Patterson Air Force Base. Stubborn, argumentative and hostile, Sonny spent more time dodging his job coach that working. The job coach soon discovered that Sonny was motivated by a paycheck and only then did both sides make real progress. Slowly, Sonny's trust in others returned.

In 1998, Sonny was promoted to supervisor of a project where he oversees the work of eight employees with disabilities. He trains, schedules, coaches, counsels and works side-by-side with them, giving constant encouragement along the way.

Today, Sonny still copes with the residual results of his disability. He has difficulty following multiple-step instructions so everything must be written down. But Sonny says: " I have a good-paying job and I work with people who appreciate what I do." He has health insurance for his family and himself. Plus, Sonny's investing in a new bank of memories made up of successful experiences, hard work, and the support of the family of friends at Goodwill.

DON MONTZ
CLINTON, MARYLAND

Don Montz has been working at the Smithsonian Institution Service Center since September of 1996. The 22-year-old works among monstrous displays, exhibits and invaluable archives while he bears the responsibility of keeping the areas clean and in good order. The Service Center is a challenging location for cleanliness. It is, after all, a whitewashed, rustic building dating back to the 1920s. Over the years, Don's good work has given him the added responsibility of managing all four floors of the building.

When he graduated from Surrattsville High School, the future didn't look this bright for Don. With his developmental disabilities, he found school itself was difficult to survive. "It was real hard for me to find a job," he says. "If it hadn't been for Melwood (the local community rehabilitation program that trained Don for his current job), I don't know what I'd be doing."

Don must love his job. In order to get to it each day, he must get up at 5 a.m., leave at 5:45 to catch the bus and metro to work where he arrives at 7:10 a.m. His route home is no easier. He leaves work at 3:30 p.m. and gets home around 5 p.m. After all, he says, "The world doesn't owe you a living...you earn it yourself."

In his free time, Don is active in his local church, loves astonomy and science fiction and plays the keyboard and organ. Ten percent of his wages goes to his church and transportation costs.

Proud of his accomplishments and his work with Melwood Training Center, Don says: "This is the first chance I've had to show the abilities I have to offer. It's the first good job I've ever had."

THOMAS BROUGHT PLENTY

RAPID CITY, SOUTH DAKOTA

As a member of the Standing Rock Sioux Tribe of Fort Yates, North Dakota, Thomas Brought Plenty lives up to his name. Thomas has phocomelia, a congenital deformity in which his limbs are underdeveloped, coupled with a form of mental retardation.

His work experience began in 1978 when Tom started to work as an envelope sealer shortly after entering the Black Hills Training and Employment Workshop in Rapid City, South Dakota. He graduated from that work quickly and moved to the wood shop where he worked as a sander, earning just thirty cents an hour. . He again quickly adapted to the task and mastered all of the duties asked of him.

One day, he appeared in the doorway of his supervisor and said "I am bored with the work I'm doing...I know I can do (more challenging) work." His supervisor was both surprised and concerned. He felt that Tom's shortened arms and distorted hands would limit him in accomplishing the tasks of banding bundles and rip cutting on a radial arm saw and he was worried for Tom's safety. The supervisor gave Tom a one-week trial period on the job. One week later, the supervisor visited the work area and was amazed— Tom had mastered all of the tasks required.

Tom next transferred to the electronics assembly area which required inserting tiny electronic components on circuit boards and then clipping their leads to within five-thousands of an inch. Once again, Tom excelled.

Tom then moved on to the JWOD contract in the Federal Building downtown. He assumed the role of team leader and established many relationships with all of the building's tenants. His smile and positive ("I can do it.") attitude won many over. When Tom moved to the Ellsworth AFB basewide JWOD custodial contract, his peers and customers celebrated his advancement but felt his loss. In August of 1997, Tom was referred to the Job Placement Team designed to find him work on his own in the community. Within one week, he was hired as a custodian overseeing work in five buildings in a local automobile dealership. On good weather days, he walks to work—a distance of five miles.

Tom plays basketball for the agency's team and attends semi-pro basketball games. This Denver Broncos' fan works with Dakota Link—an agency that provides assistive technology and research for accommodating work stations for individuals with disabilities. True to his name, Thomas brings plenty to his co-workers, to his neighbors and many friends.

JOANNA RICHARDSON

ROCHESTER, NEW YORK

Joanna is no stranger to work. She landed her first job at age 13. She holds an associate's degree from Monroe Community College and she has even worked as a medical secretary at several companies. In 1986, Joanna was employed by the Association for the Blind and Visually Impaired—at Goodwill Industries of Greater Rochester. Both the organization and Joanna have grown as a result of the partnership.

Since 1993, she has operated a 14-ton mill cutting machine affectionately called the "guillotine." As a mill cutter operator working on a Javits-Wagner-O'Day Project, Joanna processes several thousand dozen of repositionable note pads each day. Her work alone keeps three packers busy and the production line moving at a steady pace. Engineers at the Goodwill facility adapted the equipment by installing several verbal output devices so she can tell its position and settings. Joanna may well be the only blind person operating such a machine in the country.

When talking about her job, Joanna says, "I feel I am...appreciated..and I'm gratified that the government has the confidence in people who are blind to manufacture products for federal use. Goodwill has given me the opportunity to seek and attain my highest level of independence."

Joanna is the proud mother of four children. She works hard to be a strong role model for them. "By working," Joanna says, "I set an example for my children, so they understand that working is the way and nothing comes easily. You get what you earn."

BARRY ROACH

BEVERLY, NEW JERSEY

Raised in a series of foster homes, Barry Roach experienced both good and bad times. Finally, he came to live with the woman he now calls his mother—in the home in which he finally found "warmth" he says. His mother also opened her doors to other foster children. It was through this arrangement that Barry found the woman who is now his wife and mother of their two children—Elizabeth and Mary Rose. "It was Halloween and Mom took in people with disabilities to help with independence.."

His wife had a job with the Occupational Training Center of Burlington County (OTC) as a bench assembly worker. Barry decided to "come along" one day, too.

As a result, Barry was also assigned to the bench assembly area but stayed there only one day before moving to OTC's recycling project where he sorted glass, plastic, tin and paper. It was apparent early on that he was extremely motivated and conscientious in all work-related areas. After working in recycling for ten weeks, he decided (on his own) that he wanted to train in the food service area so that he could go to work at McGuire Air Force Base.

One day he received a phone call from nearby Trenton, New Jersey, and discovered that he had five brothers and six sisters that he never knew he had. It seems that they had all been placed in different foster homes. Several of the older siblings had begun a search to find the missing family members. Barry was the last one to be found.

Barry is an accomplished artist specializing in airbrush works and loves to play "street drums." He credits his job for his "strong attitude and it's made me able to stand up for myself." His job has also brought him the money to buy a home and a car so he can drive up and visit his brothers and sisters in Trenton.

JOLITA SAMUELS
WASHINGTON, DC

Jolita Samuels' successful career has come as a result of a number of progressive achievements. She first entered training at the Melwood Training Center through the Job Training Partnership Act Program. Upon graduation from that program, she became a crew member on Melwood's grounds maintenance team. Her success there led to her working as part of a cooperative work unit at the National Zoo in Washington, DC. Each of these jobs contributed skills and knowledge that led her to employment on a Javits-Wagner-O'Day project at the Naval Research Laboratory (NRL) in Washington. The NRL's main mission is to conduct intensive scientific research and advanced technological development as it relates to engineering, space, environmental science and advance development programs. The job carries a security clearance requirement with it.

Jolita's individual responsibilities include maintaining the office areas on one floor of the Navy's laboratory. Among the offices she must clean are those of the top officials there - the Commanding Officer, Inspector General and the Director of Research. Her work requires the highest standards.

The highly-charged diminutive dynamo was born and raised in the nation's capital. No one really knows her age because she flat-out refuses to tell anyone. Even her family—she has three sisters and two brothers—don't know her age. "They get it messed up..." she says shyly. One clue could be her eleven-year-old daughter, Damiti.

"Working with people and helping people out" is one of the reasons she likes her job. Another is the fact that her job lets her pay bills and "buy gifts for my daughter."

93

DAVID SCHAFEBOOK

BETHLEHEM, PENNSYLVANIA

David Bruce Schafebook comes from a very strong and loving family. His father is an engineer with the Bethlehem Steel Corporation. His mother is a nurse at a nearby hospital. His sister, Jill, is a Special Education teacher and another sister is a Speech Therapist in Maryland. Due to his family's support and his own volition, David was able to complete his education with the Bethlehem School District Vo-Tech program.

After graduation, he began working at the Kurtz Training Center—a division of the Lehigh Valley Association for Retarded Citizens. He was assigned to a custodial work crew as part of a Javits-Wagner-O'Day project. Following this training and experience, David found work at the local grocery store—ShopRite Food Markets, Inc. He's been there seven years and he still loves it. Reports from his supervisors indicate that ShopRite loves him, too.

In 1983, David entered into a group home environment under the residential services of LARC. He and his two roommates and staff have become an extended family.

David enjoys a very active social schedule that includes family visits, picnics, bowling, movies, sports events, and vacations. Indeed, he's made two trips to Canada and upper New York State over the last few years.

95

ALBERT SCURO

ORLANDO, FLORIDA

Growing up in Depression-era Pittsburgh (Pennsylvania), Albert Scuro was the oldest son of Italian immigrants. By the time he entered school, Albert spoke Italian but could not understand English. Teachers blamed his academic failures on the language barrier until an astute teacher realized that Albert could not see the blackboard.

While Albert's blindness limits him from seeing beyond three feet, nothing prevents him from seeing human potential. He helped support his family by selling newspapers at a corner newstand for forty years. He earned a penny a paper, sometimes selling 200 papers a day. In 1982, he and his brothers moved to Florida, where Albert cared for his nieces and nephews until they had finished college.

So, at 64, when most people retire, Albert began what he refers to as his "first real job"—custodial work at the Orlando Naval Training Center. Initially reluctant to commit to the job, he feared his disability would prevent him from performing the job to his own high expectations. There were days when he wanted to quit. But once familiar with his surroundings and coworkers, he never looked back. Albert continued working primarily because his coworkers many of whom also had disabilities, relied on him for his words of encouragement. He mastered skills, including the management of the dishwashing area and he earned the respect of his co-workers, counselors and supervisors. "Albert brings out the best in people " says Food Services Director Larry Fulton.

On Mother's Day in 1996, Albert suffered a stroke. For an entire day, he lay on his apartment floor, paralyzed and unable to summon help. On Monday, a neighbor realized Albert needed emergency care. After eight weeks of physical therapy and coupled with his emotional grit, Albert regained all he lost—his speech, mobility and physical strength. By August, he returned to work while the entire shift waited for him around the time clock. When Albert arrived, they all cheered as he reported for duty.

WILLIE SMITH

DES MOINES, IOWA

Willie Smith had his first psychiatric episode at the age of 19. Prior to this incident, Willie's future looked limitless. Upon admission to a psychiatric hospital, Willie was withdrawn, experiencing visual and auditory hallucinations, and admitted to paranoia toward family members. Doctors were forced to use four-way restraints to allow them close enough to treat him. He responded to medication positively and was discharged with a recommendation to participate in a rehabilitation program.

In March of 1985, Willie began his training at Goodwill Industries of Central Iowa. He expressed an interest in learning how to perform custodial work. After an initial assessment and training, Willie was transferred to work as a custodian on a JWOD contract at the Federal building in downtown Des Moines. Within a short period of time, Willie demonstrated the ability to learn his job and to take on additional responsibilities. After being placed as an Office Team Leader at the Federal building, then at the U.S. Courthouse as the Day Office Custodian, Willie was the natural choice to step up as Supervisor at the Pleasant Hill City Complex. This complex houses the city hall, fire department, police department, citiy council chambers and the public library. As a result of his outgoing personality and dedication there, Willie has built an excellent rapport with all of the department heads and even the Mayor.

Willie has needed occasional psychiatric hospitalizations since his initial bout with schizophrenia. He states that being able to know that there is a job waiting for him is one of the key elements in his recovery. Willie believes that the Goodwill Janitorial Program and JWOD have helped him gain the self-esteem and employment stability he needed to feel good about himself. He believes that he is a contributing member of society. Willie is continually striving to meet his goals to be the best custodian possible.

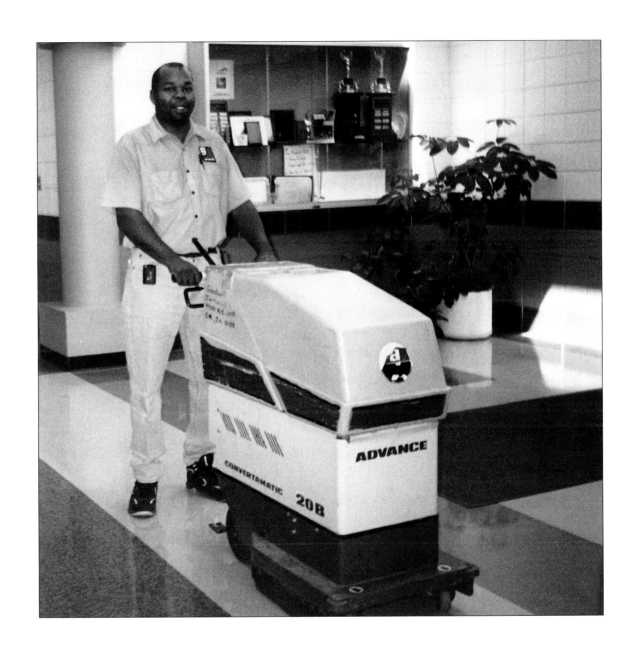

ARNOLD STANDIFER

ANCHORAGE, ALASKA

Arnold Standifer was born in May of 1961 in Tyonek, Alaska, to a native Alaskan family. Overwhelmed by the fact that Arnie was diagnosed with a seizure disorder, cerebral palsy and mental retardation, his family sought a program of scheduled treatment through an Anchorage Hospital. During treatment, Arnie was moved to a foster home, and shortly thereafter, Arnie "adopted" his new parents—Ted and Ellen Whip. The support he received from his new family helped to speed Arnie's therapy and rehabilitation.

In 1981, he moved to a group home run by Hope Cottages in Anchorage. He graduated from Barlett High School in 1982, and started with Anchorage Specialized Education and Training Services (ASETS) later that year. He was assigned to the Work Activity Center's telephone refurbishing operation. Working successfully on that project, Arnie was subsequently transferred to the bindery operation at the community rehabilitation program.

Wanting a more challenging position, Arnie would continually approach the ASETS staff about "getting a community job" for him. In 1990, he got his opportunity—with a trial placement at the Elmendorf Air Force Base Commissary on a Javits-Wagner-O'Day project. Getting the position was easy—compared to making it work successfully. After all, Arnie used a wheelchair and the problems of logistics of performing custodial and shelf stocking work in a crowded commissary at first seemed insurmountable.

While an electric wheelchair afforded Arnie greater mobility, the commissary, crowded with boxes of groceries and other products, was, at first, a nightmare obstacle course to maneuver. In addition, trying to manage custodial chores from a wheelchair also presented a set of different challenges. However, with the help of the staff at ASETS, and some clever rehabilitation engineering efforts, Arnie mastered these and other challenges.

The stability of the job at the Air Base has given Arnie the chance to enhance his lifestyle. He enjoys Friday night dances sponsored by the Arc of Alaska. His handle on the CB radio is "Wheelchair kid." He schedules his own transportation. Moreover, Arnie continues to advocate for himself and others. Perhaps his biggest role as an advocate, however, is the fact that he is living proof that the only true limits that prevent independence and growth are often those that are self-imposed.

Today, Arnie has taken on more responsibilities at his job. He stocks the shelves at the commissary in addition to still doing custodial work. He was recently recognized for 15 years of service with ASETS. Working with his family, relatives and ASETS team, Arnie is presently on a path toward another dream—buying his own condo. He's eager to live on his own and renovations are being made so that he will soon move in.

JOHN SWANCUTT

LA CROSSE, WISCONSIN

John is in his 21st year of working at ORC Industries in La Crosse, Wisconsin. During his career at the community rehabilitation program, John has worked successfully at almost every job in the plant's operation. He has been an assembler and general laborer in the woodshop and has worked in the sewing department on the wet-weather ponchos—a Javits-Wagner-O'Day product used by U.S. servicemen and women throughout the world. John has worked in the assembly department and as a machine operator, where he attached grommets onto the poncho hoods. He also has worked on military items like panel markers used in the Gulf War, Dixie Cup Navy hats, and mos recently, improved rainsuit parkas and trousers.

Swancutt has developmental disabilities which according to his records, create "psychomotor difficulties and an inability to spacially visualize and conceptualize information." Translating this to everyday language, his problems are manifested in poor motor coordination and slower reaction times. Thus, it's hard for John to learn new tasks, retain information, and produce at a constant rate. John also has speech impairment, decreased standing tolerance, and low vision.

In spite of these problems, however, John is persistent, optimistic, has maintained an excellent attitude and shows little sign of slowing down. He lives independently in an apartment in the home of his sister and his brother-in-law. They provide the minimal supports that John needs. He independently shops for groceries, prepares meals, and cleans up. His hobbies include playing the drums and various sports. He is an active participant in the Special Olympics and has a case full of medals and ribbons to prove it.

The stability offered by the JWOD work allows him to learn and task and to do it well. Does he like his work? Maybe the answer lies in the fact that his average attendance rate during the past 10 years is a phenomenal 97%. John is almost impossible to discourage and he takes great pride in achieving goals he sets for himself.

Due to John's continued excellence in the workplace, ORC has continually sought work for John in a supported employment environment. Despite a positive assessment and an exhaustive job search, nothing has been found which serves John's needs and abilities like the work on the JWOD project. John's goals for the future are to continue working for ORC. He hopes to have the opportunity to work on the grommet machine again.

One ORC staff member perhaps describes John best as "the man who's never had a bad day." Asked recently to identify his own best qualities and skills, John Swancutt answered: "being honest...being a gentleman..."

103

DOUGLAS TAKSAR

ARLINGTON, VIRGINIA

Taking it one step at a time might as well be Douglas Taksar's motto. When he was an infant, his parents were told that he would never ride a bike or drive a car because of his developmental disability. In fact, they said, he would probably not make it past the third or fourth grade. Today, the 25-year-old works full time as a correspondence clerk for the Office of Executive Secretariat at the Environmental Protection Agency (EPA) in Washington, D.C. He also lives in his own apartment, and receives tutoring in reading and writing through the Literacy Council.

Doug is responsible for opening and logging incoming mail for the Administrator and the Deputy Administrator. He gained the necessary job training and communications skills necessary to seek employment following his work with the Javits-Wagner-O'Day Program and Fairfax Opportunities Unlimited in Alexandria, Virginia. From 1992-1995, Doug worked as a supply clerk on a JWOD contract.

He found out about the government vacancy on his own. "Doug took the initiative to pursue the paperwork and necessary interviews (with the assistance of his FOU employment specialist)" says Yvonne Carter, Doug's FOU Site Manager at the EPA supply store. Doug's current supervisor at EPA's Executive Office is pleased with his performance. "Doug is dedicated to doing the job right and to learning new skills and teaching them to others," she says. He consistently works beyond the call of duty. On evenings and weekends, he works part time at a local hardware store in the warehouse to earn extra money.

In 1995, while leaving work, Doug and a coworker, ignoring danger to themselves, rushed to the aid of a woman being attacked in a nearby alley. Their actions saved the woman. Doug received a "Hero" award from the EPA for his role in this incident.

Doug's future plans include being an advocate for people with disabilities. He's spoken to a variety of community organizations and recently testified before the Senate Subcommittee on Employmnet and Training about the role rehabilitation has played in his life. At all forums, Doug's constant message about people with disabilities is: "We are limited in some ways, but we are strong in many other ways."

SARAH TEMPLE

MILFORD, DELAWARE

In 1964, Mary Jane Temple discovered that she had contracted German Measles. Ordinarily, this is an illness of small concern. However, Mary Jane was pregnant with her daughter, Sarah, and the outcome was uncertain, since it was known that rubella can bring harm to a baby. At the medical specialists first look, it seemed that Sarah's only disability was her deafness. After time, though, it became clear that Sarah had multiple disabilities. In truth, says Mary Jane Temple today, "There were as many diagnoses as there were doctors who examined her." Sarah was followed by Children's Hospital of Philadelphia which did a great deal of work with rubella babies at that time. Her parents discovred that Sarah didn't like and couldn't adjust to change. She needed a stable and predictable pattern to her life. With eight children in a household, this was difficult to accomplish. Soon, Sarah was placed with nearby Elwyn Inc. which offered a full-range of services and numerous job training and JWOD projects. From age 6 to age 21, Sarah lived, learned and worked at Elwyn. She worked on everything from assembly work to an administrative aide's responsibilities.

Following Elwyn, Sarah moved on to the Stokely Center in Georgetown, Delaware. Her behavior had changed to one of abusive outbreaks and disruptive actions. Due to the fact that she is non-verbal for the most part, it was difficult to provide her with the appropriate care and services. Sarah's behavior didn't improve much then and eventually, she found herself at the Kent Sussex Industries. There, her job coaches worked on her behavior and also took the definitive step to place her in a group home. "The people there have been wonderful. Sarah's a different person." her mother says. In cooperation with The Chimes, Inc., Sarah became part of the custodial crew at Dover Air Force Base and the results have been amazing. She has the stability that needs to succeed. "I believe she's working at her peak and she feels really productive. She loves her job and the sense of belonging it gives her." her mother reports. "She really doesn't get excited about anything but work and shopping."

107

TERRY THOMAS

OKLAHOMA CITY, OKLAHOMA

The trauma of Terry Thomas' birth almost cost her her life.

As a result of the severe difficulties she experienced during birth, Terry's vision was damaged. At age three, she suffered another shock—a severe case of measles left her permanently hearing impaired. Today, she remembers her childhood as a constant struggle, trying to cope with her disabilities and her own social insecurities. To make things worse, Terry was uprooted often due to the family's relocations as a result of her father's job.

Despite all of these upheavals, however, Terry was determined to succeed. Her mother helped by educating her at home. But it was in High School that Terry found herself. She was provided with large print materials, learned to read braille, and gained self-confidence. She excelled academically and went on to college. She married and began her own family. Terry was determined to never look back.

But the marriage failed and, suddenly, Terry was faced with the support of her two daughters alone. In need of dependable income, Thomas sought employment at the Oklahoma League and found it as a machine operator on a Javits-Wagner-O'Day project. Given the opportunity to establish herself again, she did just that. She has been working at the League since 1983. Her supervisor calls her dependable, hardworking and always willing to help out where needed.

In addition to work, Terry is involved actively in her church and volunteers on behalf of the Moore Lions Club in Oklahoma City. She is a member of the Women's Mission Union raising funds to support mission efforts worldwide.

GEORGE TILLETT

CLEVELAND, OHIO

George Tillett works as part of the custodial crew at the Anthony Celebreeze building in downtown Cleveland. He has been a part of this project since 1988 when he was employed through a Javits-Wagner-O'Day project and the Vocational Guidance Services (VGS). The federal building is a huge cleaning project with over 1 million square feet to clean and maintain. George's primary responsibilities rest on two floors.

"I do 60 bathrooms a day, ladies and guys. I love to clean. I really enjoy it. Nobody gets nothing on the ground when I'm working. All of my tenants tell me that nobody cleans better than George." And the truth is few do unless George's disability causes him problems.

George's disability is mental illness. The importance of support services for George in the work environment are best demonstrated by one defining moment. One day, George suddenly felt pressures mounting on him. He had a panic attack of major pro-portions. George ran to a window sill on the 17th floor of the building. A VGS supervisor, Jim Hudak, ran to George's side and counseled him for a few minutes. Shortly thereafter, George and Jim walked quietly out of the building. "I simply said 'Let's go down to the street and see if things look better from down there" says Hudak.

Despite the scare, when tenants on George's floor were planning to move their offices up to another floor in the building, they specifically asked for George to be a part of their crew and to move with them. "They (the tenants) are like a family to me," he says "They really care about what I do and about cleaning. I try not to miss a day. I really love to work."

George lives with his mom and helps her with expenses. In addition, he uses some of his earnings to take kids rollerskating. He has a pet ferret and iguana. He's also into rollerblading and in the summer does tricks like "360s and splits" on the sidewalk in front of the building on his lunch hour.

111

MOSES TITTLE

WICHITA, KANSAS

Quiet and unassuming, Moses, his wife and his sixteen-year-old son, Mansfield, enjoy a traditional lifestyle. Moses serves as the breadwinner and has for years. Born in Arkansas, Moses had a normal childhood, attended school and helped with farm work. After high school, he got a job at a sawmill. His work assignment there was to catch strips of boards as logs emerged from the initial sawing operation. When he had been on the job barely two and a half weeks, he suffered a severe injury to a finger on his left hand. The surgery to repair that injury resulted not only in the loss of the finger, but also brain damage from a lack of adequate oxygen during the procedure. Moses became a quadraplegic and temporarily, completely blind. He was enrolled in a series of special training programs and moved through a variety of rehabilitation foundations and programs.

Showing abilities to perform industrial work assignments, Moses moved to a JWOD project for the General Services Administration at Center Industries in Wichita. Over the years, Moses was transferred to the Boeing Window Frame area. A drilling fixture has been modified to allow Moses to drill window frames for Boeing 737 and 777 airplanes. This job requires a higher skill level than the previous positions that Moses has held and he is, not surprisingly, doing an excellent job. He continues to exceed the standards set for the job.

Moses met his wife at the Urban Residential Center, a housing facility for people with disabilities. They have been married for nineteen years. Thirty-three years after that accident, Moses has regained part of his sight, seeing light and dark and the location of large objects. The normalcy of the Tittles' lives is a tribute to Moses' quiet persistence.

Moses intends to retire after his sixteen-year-old son graduates from high school. His disability has progressed over the years and he is no longer ambulatory and requires a scooter for mobility. Other than work, he keeps busy doing things with his son. He is active in his church.

DIM VAN TRAN

HOLLAND, MICHIGAN

Dim Van Tran never owned a wheelchair and because he had a disability, he therefore, wasn't allowed to attend school. He wasn't permitted to hold a job either but that didn't stop him from dreaming about one. His sisters taught him to read in the evenings.

When his family was scheduled to emigrate to the United States, the eighteen-year-old Dim felt his dream would actually come true. At the very last minute though, he learned that only he would be allowed to emigrate. Dim had a tough decision to make: stay with the comfort of his family and friends or take a risk and leave everything he knew to pursue a dream among strangers in a foreign culture.

He arrived in the United States from Vietnam almost seven years ago. Church sponsors placed him with a foster family, helped him obtain a wheelchair and enrolled him in English as a second language class.

Through Michigan Rehabilitation Services, Dim began evaluation and work training at Kandu Industries. Because he had no use of his legs and had never had a wheelchair, Dim had developed a great deal of upper body strength. This made transfers from his wheelchair to a high stool at his work station almost effortless. He quickly taught the Kandu staff the most efficient way to set up jobs on the Javits-Wagner-O'Day contract to best meet his needs. Dim took a leadership role with the team working to train him. The quiet young man with the shy sense of humor quickly won the respect of staff and coworkers alike. Dim's work in his English classes resulted in a role for him as translator with other non-English-speaking people in the training classes.

Since his employment with Kandu, Dim has continued to increase his earnings and as a result, he pays taxes, pays for his own room and board and has purchased a car fitted with hand controls. His plans now include a trip back to Vietnam to visit his relatives.

After four years of working on the JWOD project, Dim was recently placed at a large office furniture manufacturer fulfilling yet another of Dim's dreams.

DEBORAH VARNER

WICHITA FALLS, TEXAS

Deborah Varner began work at the Work Services Corporation in July of 1971. She progressed through a variety of different jobs in the workshop and as a result, was selected as an employee in the first JWOD full food service contract way back in 1981. Deborah's job responsibilities include serving meals to patrons, cutting and displaying pastry, bussing tables, operation of a commercial dishwashing machine, and general custodial duties in the dining hall. As an experienced and versatile employee, she has assisted in the orientation and training of numerous new employees over the past 17 years by passing on those things she's learned.

Deborah is a champion of self-advocacy programs for people with disabilities. She has served as President of local and State of Texas Chapters of People First, the self-advocacy arm of the Arc of Texas. She received the Arc of Texas citizenship award in 1988. Deborah also served on the Steering Committee for Project Jobs, an employment program sponsored by the Texas Planning Council for Developmental Disabilities. She has even lobbied for disability issues at the Texas State Legislature and the US Congress. She has served on the local MHMR Advisory Committee and on the Burkburnett Independent School District Advisory Committee for Special Education.

This human dynamo who is tall on commitment stands only (and barely) five feet tall. Deborah's favorite hobbies include reading, sports and "anything to do with kids."

SAM WATLINGTON

NORFOLK, VIRGINIA

Sam Watlington was born in Charleston, West Virginia, in 1959. Born with Down Syndrome, he attended public schools until 1981. From August of 1981 until December 1985 , Sam worked in a program at the Louise Eggleston Center in Norfolk. From December of 1985 through 1990 Sam worked in an enclave program at Norfolk State University where he trained in grounds maintenance jobs. In 1990, he transferred to a mobile work crew performing general custodial duties there. Then in 1992, Sam transferred to a job in one of the first JWOD laundry services projects in the country. The enormity of this project was overwhelming: to manage the entire laundry services for the Portsmouth Naval Hospital —some 8000 pounds a day.

As a laundry worker, Sam operates a towel folding machine and also handles the rough/dry folding. He packs laundry carts—a task that only a handful of workers are able to perform—and is able to work independently in the blanket folding area when the lead worker is absent. But since his transfer to the laundry project, his family has noticed that Sam demonstrates greater independence in a number of areas. Sam lives with his parents and thrives with the comfort that his very supportive family brings. His parents, one brother and two sisters keep him motivated and focused.

Sam maintains his own bank account. With his earnings from the laundry job he pays for his transportation to and from work. He also used some of his pay to buy his own computer. Two of his siblings are teachers and are assisting him in selecting and operating various computer programs. Among his favorites are those which help him with his reading skills. He also routinely purchases bus tickets to visit his sister who lives two hours away in Richmond. Sam makes the bus ride on his own.

Through the JWOD work, Sam has increased his productivity and his pay over the years by 412%! What else does he do with his money? "I like to go to the movies. For fun, I like to help my Daddy cut grass, work with leaves and help my Mom with the laundry … not this laundry" he explains.

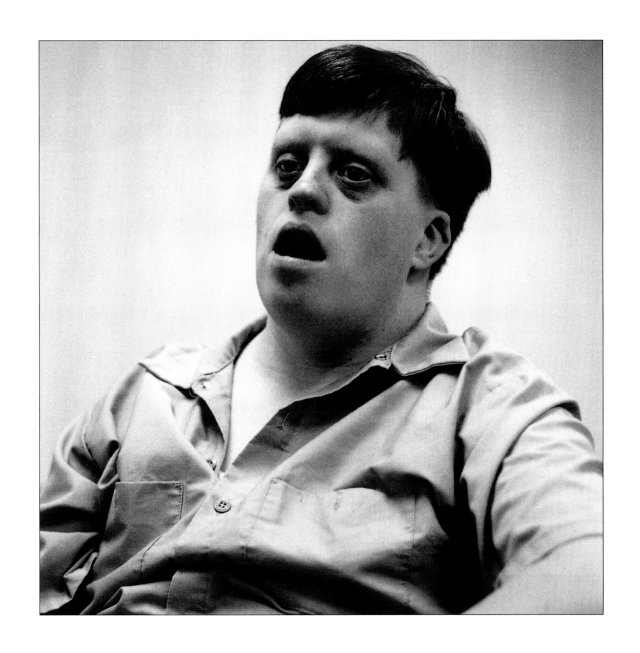

119

GAIL WHRITENOUR

ALEXANDRIA, VIRGINIA

The winter of 1994 brought severe, treacherous weather to the Washington, DC, area. Ice storms prevailed. Countless offices were shut down and on several occasions, the entire Federal Government closed its doors. The thing that several people at the Environmental Protection Agency (EPA) mailroom remember most, however, is that their colleague, Gail Whritenour, came to work every day in spite of those storms. One of Gail's supervisors reported: She made the rest of us feel bad when she came to work and some of us didn't."

Yet, getting to work is no easy task for Gail (although you'll never hear her say that!). She has to take a bus and two metro trains to her stop at the Waterside Mall near the EPA offices. Mastering mass transit in the nation's capital is never easy, but with the extra challenge of utilizing a wheelchair it can be particularly daunting—for most everyone except Gail.

Gail works for Fairfax Opportunities Unlimited (FOU) on the Javits-Wagner-O'Day project. Her association with FOU began in the late 1980s when she sought employment opportunities and training there. It seemed destined for oblivion, though, when in 1991, she was forced to undergo reconstructive surgery on her hip which had degenerated from years of improper alignment. Compounding her difficulties is the fact that Gail is faced with spastic cerebral palsy. Following surgery, she began ardous physical therapy. In October of 1993, Gail returned to work at the mailroom.

Gail's productivity is another testament to both her conscientiousness and her determination. At the time of her return to work, the spasms in her hands limited her production to eight pieces of mail a day. Gail's unwillingness to accept this as her "best" and her consistent dedication to try harder, inspired her supervisor to work with Gail to find appropriate adaptive devices and techniques to stabilize her hand movements. A computer keyguard eliminated inadvertent striking of multiple keys and a higher resolution screen compensated for Gail's vision limitations. With these modifications and her personal commitment to succeed, Gail steadily improved her work. Currently, she is among the highest producers in her enclave. In one entire year, only two pieces of mail processed by Gail were flagged.

Married and living in her own apartment, Gail's professional and personal achievements have enhanced the quality of her life and the lives of those who work with her every day.

Acknowledgments

My personal thanks to Zelda Langdale, Mary Jones, Larissa Timmerberg, Chuck Tasca, Beverly Milkman and Kim Zeich for their help in editing and researching this book. Thanks to Joshua Javits for being so accessible and for carrying on his father's legacy so easily while building his own. Thanks to Dan McKinnon and Bob Dupwe for supporting and embracing this project. Thanks, too, to all of my colleagues at NISH who believe so fervently and work so tirelessly in promoting employment of people with severe disabilities nationwide. Thanks to all of the folks at the following community rehabilitation programs whose work, energies and daily triumphs underscore the achievements in this book:

Abilities Unlimited
ASETS
Black Hills Workshop and Training Center
Center Industries, Inc.
The Chimes, Inc.
Consolidated Products & Services, Inc.
Cooperative Workshops
CW Resources, Inc.
Easter Seals of Western Pennsylvania
Expanco, Inc.
Fairfax Opportunities Unlimited
Goodwill Industries of Central Florida
Goodwill Industries of Central Iowa
Goodwill Industries of Greater Rochester
Goodwill Industries of Miami Valley
Hope Enterprises, Inc.

Houston County Association for
    Exceptional Citizens
Kandu Industries, Inc.
LARC, Inc.
Louise Eggleston Center
Lighthouse Industries in Long Island City
Melwood Training Center
Minnesota Diversified Industries, Inc.
N. Louisiana Goodwill Industries
New Jersey Association for the Blind
Occupational Training Center of
    Burlington County
Opportunity Resources, Inc.
Opportunity Village
ORC
Pioneer Adult Rehabilitation Center

Pride Industries
RCI, Inc.
San Antonio Lighthouse for the Blind
Southeastern Kentucky Rehab Industries
Tempe Center for Habilitation
The Arc of Montgomery County
Tommy Nobis Center
Toolworks, Inc.
Tresco Inc.
Tri-Development Center
Virginia Industries for the Blind
Vocational Guidance Services, Inc.
Vocational Opportunities Center
Wichita Industries and Services for the Blind
Work Services Corporation

Photo Credits

All photographs in this book are by Linda Sullivan Schulte with the following acknowledgments.
Photos courtesy of: